Learning from the Experts

Learning from the Experts

Teacher Leaders on Solving America's Education Challenges

Edited by

Celine Coggins
Heather G. Peske
Kate McGovern

HARVARD EDUCATION PRESS
CAMBRIDGE, MASSACHUSETTS

Educ.
LB
1025.3
.L415
2013

Copyright © 2013 by the President and Fellows of Harvard College

All rights reserved. No part of this publication may be reproduced or transmitted in any form or by any means, electronic or mechanical, including photocopy, recording, or any information storage and retrieval systems, without permission in writing from the publisher.

Library of Congress Control Number 2013941191

Paperback ISBN 978-1-61250-624-1
Library Edition ISBN 978-1-61250-625-8

Published by Harvard Education Press,
an imprint of the Harvard Education Publishing Group

Harvard Education Press
8 Story Street
Cambridge, MA 02138

Cover Design: Deborah Hodgdon
Cover Photo: Ali Dorman Fernandez/Teach Plus

The typefaces used in this book are Minion and ITC Symbol BT.

CONTENTS

Acknowledgments ix

Introduction

Who Are the Real Experts?—Why We Should Ask Teachers How to Fix Our Schools 1
CELINE COGGINS

1 Creating and Using Data in Schools

Framing the Issue 5
ROSS WIENER

The Quantified Student: A "Bad Teacher" Rethinks Data Use 7
SUJATA BHATT

Unacknowledged Truths: Testing Speaks—Are We Listening? 10
MICHELLE MORRISSEY

The Right Conversation to Be Having: Why Student Growth Data Matters 13
KYLE HUNSBERGER

Response 16
ROSS WIENER

2 Ensuring Equitable Access to Great Teachers

Framing the Issue 21
KATI HAYCOCK AND SARAH ALMY

Moving the Whole School Forward: Talented Teachers for Turnaround Schools 24
ERIN DUKESHIRE AND LISA GONCALVES LAVIN

Response 36
KATI HAYCOCK AND SARAH ALMY

3 Measuring Teacher Effectiveness

Framing the Issue 39
JASON KAMRAS

Satisfactory? Me?—Giving New Teachers the Support They Deserve 41
STEPHANIE WIDMER

High IMPACT: It's the Feedback That Adds Value 43
DWIGHT DAVIS

Urgency Breeds Anxiety: The Challenge of Building Teacher Trust 46
PETER TANG

Response 53
JASON KAMRAS

4 Building a Performance-Driven Profession

Framing the Issue 55
CELINE COGGINS AND LINDSAY SOBEL

From New Teacher to Teacher Activist: What I Learned from "Mr. Miller" 58
TINA C. AHLGREN

Leaving Cherie: One Teacher's Experience of Last In, First Out 62
JEANETTE MARRONE

Response 66
CELINE COGGINS AND LINDSAY SOBEL

5 Engaging Early Career Teachers in the Union

Framing the Issue 69
PAUL TONER

From the Classroom to the Big Picture: Why I Changed My Mind About Teacher Unions 72
KAREN L. MCCARTHY

Caught in the Middle Versus Finding the Middle Ground: What's Best for the Children of Chicago? 79
GINA CANEVA

Response 83
PAUL TONER

6 Building School Leadership That Facilitates Great Teaching

Framing the Issue 87
BENJAMIN FENTON AND TERRENCE KNEISEL

I Wasn't Ready to Stop Improving: Why Irreplaceable Teachers Need Irreplaceable Leaders 89
ALLISON FRIEZE

Putting My Beliefs into Practice: Principal Leadership Makes the Difference 92
AUDREY HERZIG JACKSON

Honoring My Mother: The Evolution of an Unlikely Educator 94
JEREMY ROBINSON

Response 99
BENJAMIN FENTON AND TERRENCE KNEISEL

7 Raising the Status of the Profession

Framing the Issue 105
EDWARD LIU

Reforming Teacher Entry and Training: Shouldn't We Hold Teachers (Like Me) to a Higher Standard? 108
MEAGHAN PETERSACK

Not My Parents' Profession: Today's Teachers Need Career Ladders 111
ERIN DUKESHIRE

Too Smart to Be a Teacher?—Let's Prove My Grandmother Wrong 114
JAIME SIEBRASE HUDGINS

Response 120
EDWARD LIU

Conclusion

Where Do We Go from Here?—Turning Teacher Voice into Action 125
KATE MCGOVERN

Notes 129

About the Editors 135

About the Contributors 137

Index 151

ACKNOWLEDGMENTS

First and foremost, the editors wish to thank the teachers who generously shared their experiences and thought-provoking solutions to the challenges tackled in these pages; and the district, union, and nonprofit leaders who placed those challenges in historical and research contexts. These contributors are all professionals working passionately to improve education—whether they work in a classroom or out—and their time and efforts are greatly valued.

This book would also have been impossible without the support of our colleagues at Teach Plus, many of whom read multiple drafts and offered their insights and questions. In particular, many thanks to Monique Burns Thompson, Alice Johnson Cain, Mike Stryer, Meghan O'Keefe, Lindsay Sobel, Anna McCallie, Ellie Eckerson, and PK Diffenbaugh for their expert feedback, ideas, and brainstorming sessions. Lastly, we wish to thank Caroline Chauncey at Harvard Education Publishing Group, who shepherded this project through multiple stages without losing faith in the value of readers' hearing from teachers on these issues.

We hope the dialogues that take place in these pages will be mirrored and multiplied in productive conversations between teachers and policy makers nationwide. If we want to find solutions to the biggest challenges facing education today, we have to start with the practitioners who face those challenges in their classrooms every day.

Earlier versions of two essays in chapter one appeared in *The Huffington Post*: "The Quantified Student: A 'Bad Teacher' Rethinks Data Use," by Sujata Bhatt and "The Right Conversation to Be Having: Why Student Growth Data Matters," by Kyle Hunsberger. "Unacknowledged Truths: Testing Speaks—Are We Listening?" by Michelle Morrissey (chapter one) appeared in a different form in *Impatient Optimists,* the blog of the Bill & Melinda Gates Foundation. An earlier version of "I Wasn't Ready to Stop Improving: Why Irreplaceable Teachers Need Irreplaceable Leaders," by Allison Frieze (chapter six), originally appeared in *The Washington Post.* Portions of "Not My Parents' Profession: Today's Teachers Need Career Ladders," by Erin Dukeshire (chapter seven), originally appeared in *The Hechinger Report.*

INTRODUCTION

Who Are the Real Experts?—Why We Should Ask Teachers How to Fix Our Schools

Celine Coggins

The teaching profession is at a crossroads. Over the past five years, both the composition of the teaching force and the expectations surrounding teachers' daily work have undergone significant changes. These shifts have been destabilizing for teaching as a whole and they provoke an important question: what is the role of teachers as leaders in solving the challenges of American education?

It is critical that we ask this question now. First, we are in the throes of a profound demographic transition. For more than forty years, baby boomers have made up the majority of the teaching force. National data from the Schools and Staffing Survey reveal that the new millennium has ushered in a new majority. As of 2008, teachers with ten or fewer years' experience constitute over 52 percent of our teaching force.[1] As this new generation becomes the new majority of the teaching force, they bring new conceptions of what it means to be a professional and what they hope for teaching as a profession. This book taps into this new majority of teachers—for their ideas, their insights, their solutions to the knotty problems of education today, and their proposals for policies and implementation strategies that will keep the most effective among them in the classrooms that need them the most.

The attitudes of teachers entering the profession today differ from those of their more senior colleagues on many issues.[2] Teachers who began their careers in the last decade have known only the No Child Left Behind era and are, to some degree, products of their environment. They are significantly more likely to report that data and standards are integral to instructional improvement. They expect to be held accountable for their students' learning and are more open to the use of student growth data to measure their impact. Now is the time to build a profession that better serves students.

As baby boomers depart, so too does the expectation that the average teacher's career in the classroom may span decades. Today, half of new teachers leave the classroom within their first three to five years, just as they are reaching their peak effectiveness. The highest rates of attrition are found in urban systems. I founded Teach Plus in 2007 to address this precise challenge by providing excellent teachers with opportunities for leadership and growth that don't require them to leave the classroom. Our organization now works with more than 11,000 teachers across the United States. Through thousands of applications to our teacher leadership programs, we have learned that these teachers have mixed feelings about leaving students. They are looking for opportunities to expand their impact while continuing their classroom teaching, but they find too few. As you'll see in the chapters of this book, serving students and leading beyond the walls of their schools are dual goals that many teachers want to take on simultaneously.

In addition to demographic changes, there have been shifts in education governance that matter to teachers and their profession. Over the past generation, states, and increasingly the federal government, have taken over a role that teachers once played. Questions about who decides what is taught and how have moved further and further from the classroom. The standards and accountability movement has had a net positive effect on students. It has elevated expectations for every child, aligned curricula, and most important, focused us on the staggering achievement gaps between low-income African American and Latino students and their more privileged peers. However, an unintended consequence of the standards movement is that it risks deprofessionalizing teaching by leaving too few decisions to actual practitioners.

Today, the introduction of Common Core State Standards and new teacher evaluation systems modeled to federal standards for funding are the latest examples of policy instruments developed far from the classroom. The jury is still out on whether these reforms will create more opportunity for, or more challenge to, advancing teachers as leaders. In order for such large-scale changes to be successful, expert educators must take on the leadership necessary to transform the practice of four million American teachers. Will these ultimately become opportunities for classroom teachers to support the development of their peers? Or will we reinforce the notion that teaching is low-skill implementation work and "promote" our best out of the classroom and away from students to lead this charge? Why not more hybrid roles for teachers to be peer observers or Common Core coaches, without leaving the classroom?

There is a specific dimension of professionalism that is not often discussed in relation to teaching. Certain characteristics distinguish professions from other forms of work. Among them are a complex and codified body of knowledge, strict standards for entry, autonomous practice, and an elevated status in society. There is healthy debate over the degree to which teaching bears these characteristics and how certain policies can enhance the professionalism of teaching.

Ownership over key problems facing the field is a hallmark of professional work. While policy leaders discuss how to elevate entry standards for teachers or pay teachers better, few suggest that teachers should be the ones leading these conversations. In most cases, actual teachers are not even invited to the table when key decisions that will affect their classroom lives are deliberated and decided. This book proposes an alternative: *If you want to figure out how to fix American schools, ask teachers.* That notion is both obvious and wildly controversial.

At Teach Plus, our primary work is to create opportunities for teachers to be leaders in solving the problems that face education at all levels of the system. This book draws upon the incredible pool of teachers who have come through our leadership programs seeking paths to do just that. Through our T3 Initiative, teacher leaders are selected and trained to support their colleagues in overcoming challenges at the instructional level. Through the Teaching Policy Fellows program and Teach Plus Network, we select, train, and activate teacher leaders to advance solutions to policy problems at the district, state, or even federal level. The pioneering teachers who are profiled in these pages have reached a sweet spot in their teaching careers: with an average of eight years in the classroom (and all between three and twelve years), they have experienced the myriad challenges of their profession but are able to maintain a fresh perspective on the possibilities for change, and they are bilingual in the languages of instruction and policy. They have developed the tools to be not only exceptional practitioners, but also knowledgeable and savvy policy advisers. They are teachers who are forging a place at the table, who are willing to accept the challenges and responsibilities of owning their profession, and whose solutions are now making a difference for kids and classrooms all over the country.

Our goal with this book is to showcase the powerful work teachers are doing to advance new ideas and advocate for practical solutions to the big, seemingly intractable systemic problems that challenge America's competitiveness as a standard-bearer for educational excellence. The book's structure mimics the conversation in which practitioners and policy makers must increasingly engage in order to best address the major problems of education and find solutions that work for teachers and for kids. In each chapter, a nonprofit organization, district, or union leader frames a key issue facing the teaching profession today. With these frameworks in place, the bulk of each chapter is composed of teachers' voices. To each issue, two or three district and public charter school teachers respond, bringing their own experiences to the table and offering ideas for how they would solve the problem at hand. Finally, each chapter is bookended by a response back to the teachers.

The work of the next generation of education reform must focus on transforming the teaching profession to allow teachers like those represented here, and their many colleagues nationwide, a greater role in shaping the decisions that affect their classrooms and students. This book marks the starting point for this next stage.

1

Creating and Using Data in Schools

FRAMING THE ISSUE

Ross Wiener

Twenty-five years of research on teacher effectiveness has established two important facts:

- Among all the variables school systems control, teachers constitute the single most influential factor in how much students learn; and
- There is tremendous variation in individual teachers' effectiveness. Reducing variability in effectiveness and increasing average performance of teachers are fundamental challenges facing public education.

Access to more useful data—at the right time, in the right form—is an essential lever for dramatically improving teaching practice. For years, policy makers have focused on accountability and incentives as the levers for reforming schools. Improving practice requires policy makers to leave this comfort zone. Research and decades of experience show that recruitment incentives, pressure for schools of education to improve, and performance pay/differentiated compensation get us only so far. Each of these can be an important strategy, but the scale of the challenge and the range of variability in classroom effectiveness require an intensive focus on improving instruction. And for this we need data.

Both policy makers and strong teachers seek data, but the data they want serves different ends. The policy maker uses data to evaluate teachers or schools to determine if a teacher or a school is effective (e.g., meeting annual accountability targets). The teacher's focus in using data is the student: how can I help this student be more successful? So what can states and districts do to shift the focus to a more student-oriented use of data? How can districts help teachers to *use data* to teach their children? What data is needed to improve teaching practice? What systems need to be in place to give teachers timely access to usable data to improve their practice?

To support improvement, data must inform teachers about both how well they're doing and how they can get better. It should include information both on outputs and outcomes (what students learn) and on inputs (what teachers and schools do). Until recently, student achievement data and/or student progress data—the former measuring absolute outcomes for students and the latter measuring student growth over the course of a school year—were not considered by evaluators in assessing teacher performance. Indeed, until the last few years, most states and districts could not connect individual teachers to their students' academic records over time, and in some states such data linking was illegal. In response to recent federal incentives and pressure, all states have now removed the legal firewall between teacher and student data. This change is a good reminder that policy plays a huge role in whether teachers have access to valuable data.

Measuring the progress and achievement of a teacher's students is not a simple proposition. After all, what constitutes evidence of learning? How can students' gains be fairly measured and attributed to individual teachers (or teams of teachers and others, where appropriate)?

Policy makers' conversations have been consumed with discussing which measures of student learning will be included in teachers' formal evaluations (a topic that will be addressed further in chapter 3). And while some of the information included in the evaluation process may be useful in helping teachers improve, some of it is neither useful nor timely when it comes to supporting teachers' development and improvement or to recognizing teaching practices that are making a difference for students. State test results, adjusted for students' prior academic performance and sometimes other variables (referred to as "value-added estimates" or "effectiveness estimates"), are increasingly being included in teachers' evaluations.

Using value-added data, where it is available, may be the most fair, objective way of including student outcomes in the formal teacher evaluation process. That said, value-added data presents significant challenges for use as a tool for improvement: it assigns an effectiveness rating compared to other teachers, but doesn't elucidate areas of strength or weakness and doesn't provide diagnostic information. What's more, only about one-third of classroom teachers have access to value-added data. We can't leave the remaining two-thirds of teachers without any measures of the effectiveness of their teaching. So we need to focus much more on the data for improving instruction. What does this look like, and where does it leave us?

THE QUANTIFIED STUDENT

A "Bad Teacher" Rethinks Data Use

Sujata Bhatt

In early 2011, in the *Washington Post*, I wrote a blog post titled "I Am a Bad Teacher," in which I questioned myself for teaching test-taking strategies to nine-year-olds. I had just instructed a student to complete all the questions on a district standardized bubble test, even ones he didn't know the answers to, and I was disgusted with a world in which adults' pursuit of data seemed more urgent than the needs of the students whose strengths and weaknesses that data was supposed to reveal. Data, I felt, was antithetical to creativity and to preparing students to discover themselves and the world.

Since writing that blog post, however, I've changed my mind. I've learned to focus not on adapting my students to the test, but rather on using the test to help meet my students' needs.

Their needs are many. I teach in Los Angeles at a Title I school. My students are largely English language learners, and our school is dotted and dashed with its share of poverty-related urgencies. In the fall of 2010, my fourth-grade class had come to me particularly unprepared. Reading, writing, subtraction, multiplication facts, focusing, doing homework, not throwing paper balls at random moments midclass: all this was a revelation to many of them (and not one they welcomed). All fall I had been plagued by the twin terrors of trying to teach them and of getting them to standardized testing proficiency. As our year-end state tests loomed and I wrote my *Washington Post* piece, it became clear to me that standardized testing was not going away anytime soon. I had to find a way to live with myself and—more important—to help my students.

Since California's standardized test for fourth graders measures skills almost all my students lacked, I analyzed its requirements, broke them down into core concepts, and then worked and reworked these concepts with the students until they felt a sense of mastery over them. My daily job consisted of finding different, creative ways of approaching, teaching, and reteaching the same core skills so that most all students could incorporate them into their cognitive toolkits.

It worked. The students succeeded wildly. They returned to me for fifth grade the following fall with heightened confidence. They saw something new in themselves: the reward of effort and the joy of success.

But there was something more. They came back to me curious about numbers and stats. They wanted to know how many more points it would take to get to the next level, how many more problems they'd need to answer correctly to get those points. They had begun to look at the test as they would a game, and they were invested in it. They understood that, because every fourth-grade public school student in the state had taken this very test, they could measure themselves against their peers. Suddenly, their view of the world became that much bigger. Testing had begun the process of networking them into the world beyond our little schoolyard. What I had once thought was antithetical to kids' discovering the world was actually helping birth them into that wider purview.

I watched these discoveries unfold, and I learned that students could gain something from standardized tests, data, and metrics. These things could be tools for students as much as they were tools for us adults.

Studies have shown a strong correlation between socioeconomic status and test scores. I don't think there's anyone who would deny that. But does this mean that we as teachers can't do anything until we solve the underlying social problems that lead to disparate opportunities and achievement?

I don't think so. I think it means we have to do two things at once.

We must—no question—change the political situation that, in California, allocates nearly $50,000 per year for each prison inmate[1] and $8,400 for each K–12 student.[2]

But I faced thirty-four fresh, if slightly pimply, faces every day last year. They couldn't afford to wait until we solve the problems of governance and poverty. They needed to be engaged, taught, and networked into the system—and at the highest possible level. If we don't work together to create pathways for our students *now*, gangs and those budding hormones certainly will.

And I've come to believe that using data is one way—among others—to do that.

The following academic year, working with the same cohort of students (plus ten new ones), I tried to find more learning opportunities that focused on data. We explored how numbers shape our understanding of ourselves and the world. We analyzed information graphics and dove into ways of presenting numerical information. We used math Web sites like TenMarks that deploy data dashboards to enable students to learn about their own learning even as they practice new skills. We entered TenMarks's six-week-long Math Madness competition, completed 71,406 problems, and placed sixth in the nation. And much of my students' enthusiasm for these activities grew from the initial connection between numbers and their own personal exertion that they discovered from standardized testing.

This year, I've yet again rejiggered my classroom; it focuses on learning as both an expansion of curiosities and competencies and as a search for holes that need plugging—all to be accomplished, in part, at my students' individual paces. To enable this differentiation, I arranged for my school to become a pilot school for TenMarks. As such, each child in grades one through five receives an individualized online math curriculum accessible anytime, anywhere. My students use the program's data dashboards to self-assess their strengths and areas of need, to advance faster than classroom curriculum (some are doing sixth- and even seventh-grade work), and to fill in the holes (some are doing third-grade "pick-up" work in addition to their present grade-level work). They love monitoring their own progress, printing out certificates that show they've mastered specific skills, and unlocking games after mastering a chunk of concepts.

Because they do so much of this online practice at home, additional class time is freed up for applying concepts in creative ways. Now, in addition to learning and practicing, we can also do deep or playful, individual or cooperative group explorations of numbers: analyses of the voter demographics of the 2008 presidential election, scale drawings of museums they'd like to build and Hershey bars they'd like to devour, and ratios of the relative sizes of the world's whale species and the planets.

I've learned from my students that it makes more sense for me to work to create *better* data than to fight data. Data analysis is an increasingly significant and empowering way of making sense of the world. Many professions use data to interpret their work and decide upon courses of action. In the high tech world, there's a growing movement called "The Quantified Self." With quantified-self models, adults use data to change habits and behaviors—to lose weight, exercise more, to calm themselves—in short, to self-assess honestly in relation to a particular competency or goal.

Our students are very open to this form of relating to the world, perhaps because so many of them already engage with games and game-related statistics. They enjoy tracking and comparing batting averages, tackles, interceptions, and rebounds, and they already keep video game stats on themselves. As teachers, why not take advantage of our students' impulse to play games and quantify? Having "learning stats" simply integrates academic competencies into our students' quantified senses of themselves and the world. Learning stats can become a driver of motivation.

For my students, perhaps the most important part of the quantified-self movement is the "self" part. Each stage of childhood is marked by increasing awareness of the self, the world, and the self in the world. In tracking themselves through numbers, my students are learning that knowledge is not something fixed in a book or next to a bubble; it is inside them and can be nurtured and built, mastered and created. A growing body of academic research has focused attention on the importance of growth mindsets, perseverance, tenacity, executive function, and social skills in school success. Through their focus on data—as well as through the freedom to spend time on cooperative group projects that data dashboards enable—my students are learning how to become masters of their own learning; they are building their learning selves. With data as one tool in our repertoire, creativity and competency come together to help students both master key skills and find themselves in the real world.

UNACKNOWLEDGED TRUTHS

Testing Speaks—Are We Listening?

Michelle Morrissey

I had lots of opinions about teaching when I was twenty-four and first stepping into the classroom in New York City's public schools. Here was one of those opinions: testing was undoubtedly, terribly bad. Bad for kids, bad for teachers, bad for schools.

It was the early days of No Child Left Behind back then—like the Wild West, but in my case, Brooklyn.

Then a funny thing happened: I prepped my students to take their high-stakes (read: BAD BAD BAD) Global History and Geography Regents Exam, and then I prepped them to take the U.S. History and Government Exam. By and large, they passed, and they passed because they had learned some history. And they took that learning very seriously, because passing those exams meant they could earn a high school diploma.

Then I moved to Massachusetts, where there is no required testing at all in history, and I miss it.

A lot of people—teachers, parents, administrators—feel that testing has been the end of all good things. It's true that the tests themselves are imperfect (it's hard to argue with talking pineapples, as we saw with last year's controversy over a nonsensical question in an eighth-grade reading exam in New York—thanks for that one, Pearson); their results largely reflect back to us our own systemic social inequalities. If misused, they can narrow the curriculum or the range of students that schools focus on. And some education advocates seem determined to create reigns of testing terror that can push teachers and administrators to lie, cheat, and steal in order to preserve their own livelihoods.

I hear these concerns, but I still can't imagine our schools without these tests. Because here's the thing, the thing that I think often goes unacknowledged: *these tests aren't very hard.* If a school isn't preparing the vast majority of its students to do well on them, that's a problem. It means that most of their students can't read, write, or do math to an extent that would certainly be unacceptable to me if it were my own child taking the test. And it shouldn't be acceptable to any of us, for anyone's kids.

We spend a lot of time worrying about whether or not our schools are turning into test-prep factories. But our real, much graver concern should be that so many parents have no choice but to send their children to schools where the vast majority of students are promoted from year to year but lack the ability to do basic math, to read at a proficient level, and to write coherent sentences. Of course, test scores are but one measure of a school's efficacy; great test scores don't equal a great school. But bad test scores are definitely a red flag, because these exams are merely basic measures of academic competency. The tests don't create pockets of lousy education—they just provide the data that show us where those pockets are. Without that data, kids will still not be able to read and write; those of us outside the schools just won't know about it.

But here's another problem—even with all the testing we're doing now, not enough of us know about it. I've seen this in my own home. Three days a week, my two kids are cared for by an extremely competent woman named Linda, herself the mother of two well-raised teenage daughters. Linda's oldest daughter, a rising senior at a very well respected and challenging school here in Boston, recently announced that she was going to go to a neighborhood Boston school for her senior year.

"What do you think?" Linda asked me.

In response, I grabbed my laptop, went to the Massachusetts Department of Education's Web site, and opened the school profiles for both Linda's daughter's current school and the one she was talking about going to.

Linda and I looked at their Massachusetts Comprehensive Assessment System (MCAS) scores together.

The prior year, 61 percent of the students in Linda's daughter's class had scored at the advanced level on their tenth-grade math exam. At the school she wanted to transfer to, only 16 percent had scored advanced, and a full 23 percent had failed the math portion completely. No one had failed the math at her daughter's current school—not a single student.

By the time we looked at the tenth-grade English language arts failure rates for the new school, Linda was definitely listening. "Oh," was all she said. And then, "She can't go there." And that was the end of it.

This is exactly the kind of parent decision making that state testing is supposed to enable, but even for a very competent parent who cares deeply about her kids' education and pays close attention to it, it took someone with eight years' experience in the classroom, a master's degree in education, and a laptop to find the data and help her interpret it by going through each point.

I love the Massachusetts Department of Education's "school and district profiles." They are incredibly informative, if you know where to look and, more important, how to interpret what you see. But how many parents, in any school district in this country, really understand terms like "AYP"? Massachusetts could lead the way by putting more parent- and family-friendly explanations on these profiles along with the data.

While education policy makers are having conversations about how, exactly, testing should be used in evaluating teachers, or which specific tests are good indicators of student achievement, parents—of all races, classes, and educational backgrounds—are floundering.

Some don't understand the fundamental purpose of testing and what it reveals about the strengths and weaknesses of the schools in their communities. Some assume, like I did as a first-year teacher, that testing takes all the joy out of learning, or will turn their children into bubble-filling automatons. Others lack information about how to access the data to make informed decisions about their kids' education.

Passing state tests should represent the bare minimum of achievement, not the end goal. And with the rollout of the Common Core and its accompanying assessments, we will (hopefully) see students asked to do more than answer multiple-choice questions, so that the tests will in fact measure higher-order thinking rather than just basic skills. But as we move forward, we need to communicate more directly and more frequently with parents about the purpose of these exams, and we also need to figure out how to democratize access to the data the exams create—by making the numbers publicly available and by providing explanations of what the numbers mean. If families don't understand what we're doing, or why, then we have a problem on our hands, and we need to fix it.

THE RIGHT CONVERSATION TO BE HAVING

Why Student Growth Data Matters

Kyle Hunsberger

I moved to Los Angeles eight years ago to become a middle school math teacher because I believed I could make an impact on the lives of young people. In the years since, my most memorable days were those in which I was able to see that impact taking place, whether it was in helping a student who was far below grade level finally master his multiplication tables, or challenging an advanced learner to read and calculate in binary code. Ultimately this is the calling of every public school teacher: to attempt to have a positive effect on the learning of each student in the incredibly diverse student body that walks through our door.

But for the most part, any sense I've had of my own efficacy as a teacher has been either anecdotal or pseudostatistical. Many former students drop by my classroom and express how much they learned there—I believe, as they do, that I had some impact on their learning trajectories. Nonetheless, state test results often showed that the highest scorers leaving my class were the same highest scorers who entered my class. It was difficult to measure exactly what impact my own teaching strategies were having.

In the last few years, school systems nationwide have begun to adopt data collection models that are designed to measure how much "value" teachers add to their students' learning. Known as "value-added models," they're intended to measure a student's growth from year to year in comparison with the growth of similar students across the district—rather than a student's absolute achievement. What's the purpose of that? Rather than relying on "apples-and-oranges" comparisons between students who enter my classroom with varying abilities and strengths, a nuanced value-added model gives me some reassurance that my impact can be measured no matter which students I teach.

The concept of a metric designed to isolate the actual effects of teaching practices is intriguing, not only for me, but for the thousands of other teachers who have always known we've made an impact, but yearn to know how much. While previously I had only been able to guess the extent to which my teaching affected my students' growth, a carefully crafted value-added metric can lend me insight into not only *how much* my teaching is impacting my students, but *which* groups of students my teaching is impacting the most (or equally important, the least). For example, it would be enlightening to learn that my teaching may greatly benefit my students with disabilities, but not so much my English language learners. This is exactly the kind of insight I need to become a better teacher.

In early 2013, my district, Los Angeles Unified, and my union, United Teachers Los Angeles, came to an agreement on an evaluation system that will take student achievement into account, along with schoolwide average value-added scores, but will leave out individual students' value-added data. While my district has opted to move away from using individual student growth data to evaluate teachers, I still believe that as we move forward nationally with using data to improve teaching practices, it is important to look at the potential of value-added models. A critical piece in this would be to ensure that student growth data is connected to meaningful opportunities for professional development geared toward helping teachers like me become even more effective. A principal who notices that a large number of his teachers demonstrate only low levels of impact on seventh-grade students might determine to focus strategic professional development opportunities geared toward seventh-grade instruction. Likewise if I, as an individual teacher, find that I need more help in meeting the needs of my English language learners, I should be able to rely on a bank of professional development options that my district has developed by learning from its best teachers.

The conversation regarding how we use student growth data is certainly in its infancy, but it is absolutely the right conversation to be having. And let's be clear: there are still many unanswered questions regarding both the reliability and the consequences of using such a measure. Research continues to offer improvements and recommendations around its implementation, and we need more of this. One such study, the Bill and Melinda

Gates Foundation's Measures of Effective Teaching project, released its culminating report in 2013, which showed that multiple-measure evaluation systems that include value-added data can be predictive not only of students' future performance on state tests, but also of their performance on more cognitively challenging assessments.[3] The report offers recommendations for how to most effectively balance value-added data with other measures of classroom practice.

Nonetheless, while I fully believe in the value of using student growth data, districts that plan to use this type of data to evaluate teachers must address concerns around both the accuracy of the metric and the potential unintended consequences that a test-based metric can create, such as the incentive to "teach to the test," or even (as, unfortunately, we have seen in some cases) to cheat. These issues ought to be starting points for powerful conversations among districts, teachers, families, and the union about not only how we measure excellence, but also what we do with that knowledge once we have it. I suspect that, in addition to improving professional learning and development options, use of this data to identify teachers with demonstrated strengths might offer new options for how districts assign teachers to schools and for the way principals assign students to teachers.

Making a positive impact on kids' education is the reason we joined this profession. A system that provides options and pathways to achieve this is one that should excite any teacher.

RESPONSE

Ross Wiener

Each of the teachers who wrote for this chapter embraces the use of student achievement data for improving teaching. This emerging consensus represents a real opportunity to make progress. But the teachers also wrestle with the potential for misuse of data, and issues of the quality of the information they have to use and access to data for teachers in nontested subjects. To honor teachers' commitment to using data for continuous improvement, policy makers need to provide high-quality, timely, actionable data to teachers from both assessments and observations.

ASSESSMENT DATA

As we learned from Sujata Bhatt's experience, regular interim assessment is one way to obtain useful data. Most school systems now have interim or benchmark assessments that are designed to inform instruction and that are more useful than annual statewide test results for the purpose of providing timely feedback to teachers. Turnaround time is usually a few days to a week. Items are designed to provide diagnostic information on students' strengths and weaknesses, and the schoolwide or systemwide administration creates a common basis for educators to diagnose weaknesses, identify effective practices, and collaborate in improvement.

Increasingly, policy makers are considering using data from these assessments as a possible "multiple measure" for teacher evaluations. While this could possibly add quality information to the evaluation mix, educators need to weigh in on whether it's important to keep data intended for improvement separate from data used for accountability.

To measure outcomes, it might also be important to supplement traditional standardized tests. Tests are inherently limited—they surely can and probably will get much better, but there's more we want to know about students' progress than test scores will tell us. To meet Common Core expectations, teachers need to focus more on students' analytic, problem-solving, and communication skills—and school systems need to support these efforts with good data on students' progress and mastery. Student writing can be an important source of this data, and systems need to establish standards and protocols to ensure consistent, rigorous expectations are applied to this data. Moreover, if we want teachers to focus on building students' character, their love of learning, and their ability to engage in rich discussions and debates regarding academic content, then we need data on what's expected and how well teachers are doing. Recent research suggests that teachers also have differential impact on these "noncognitive" aspects of learning, and that developing students' strengths in these areas is a critically important complement to building core academic knowledge.[4] We need data that teachers can use to help students achieve in these areas as well.

OBSERVATION DATA

Observations against a set of clearly articulated standards for teaching practice give teachers (and school systems) essential information about the quality of instruction and can provide rich data beyond what tests can provide about areas where teachers need support or improved teaching practices. There is an unfortunate history of the observation process being only a perfunctory one from which teachers receive no useful data. Feedback and guidance has been only sometimes given, has been highly inconsistent, and has not been well aligned to professional development and growth opportunities. This history has undermined the development of a common understanding of good practice and a shared vocabulary for discussing it.

But this is changing rapidly. States and districts are revisiting and refining teaching standards to explicitly articulate the system's expectations for teachers' practice, providing the foundation for data on teaching practices and their relationship to student achievement.

As they do this, policy makers need to focus intently on building the capacity and the will to provide not only more feedback, but more accurate feedback to teachers. Even in places that have invested significantly in training and certifying observers, scores in the field are inflated to the point where few teachers are getting critical feedback on areas that need improvement. This undermines the quality and usefulness of the data. Measures for the quality and actionability of feedback provided to teachers need to be developed—most school systems do not currently have such measures in place.[5] A further possibility for increasing both the scope and potentially the accuracy of observation data is to take advantage of experienced, effective teachers themselves as observers of their peers. This would create hybrid roles that would allow teachers who have proven their expertise to remain in the classroom part-time while serving as trained observers.

IMPLICATIONS FOR POLICY MAKERS

In addition to finding ways to give teachers the data they need to improve, policy makers need to address a set of related responsibilities. First, the data has to measure the most important learning outcomes. This applies to summative as well as diagnostic measures. State policies that have underinvested in the quality of assessments undermine the goal of data-driven decision making and do not adequately encourage instruction that leads to deeper learning, comprehension, and mastery. Although multistate Common Core–aligned assessments are in development, there is still an urgent need to improve the quality of interim/diagnostic assessments so teachers have reliable, high-quality data for planning and collaboration.

In addition to creating data, school systems create the conditions for using data. Common planning time and support for professional learning communities should be significant investments if teachers are expected to use data to improve. In the landmark three-year Measures of Effective Teaching study, the Bill and Melinda Gates Foundation found that approximately half of the teachers in the study struggled with "using assessments in instruction."[6] Observers/coaches need training not only in accurately rating teacher strengths and weaknesses, but also in having courageous, constructive conversations that guide professional growth. Supervisors need to model this for teachers so teachers can model it for students. And school systems need to develop measures for assessing the efficacy of the billions of dollars that are spent on formal "professional development" activities, which run the gamut from vital assistance to abysmal distraction.

An important, often overlooked, source of this data is teachers themselves. Surveys (of parents, students, and other teachers) are quickly being adapted to be used in teacher evaluations and can provide useful information to teachers about others' perceptions. Policy makers need to create measures that allow teachers to provide feedback on the support and supervision they receive. Research from the Chicago Consortium on School Research establishes trust as an essential element in sustained instructional improvements;[7] policy makers can't create trust, but they can set the expectation, measure its presence or absence in schools, and respond to the data.

If system leaders and administrators are responsible for supporting teachers' development, how are they accountable for that support? Without data assessing the quality of support teachers receive, too much responsibility inevitably falls on individual teachers to make up for what are system-level deficiencies. Aspire Public Schools, a charter school network, asks teachers and other personnel to complete extensive surveys and use the information to make improvement plans for schools and for the system.[8] Every principal, supervisor, and coach is rated by the teachers they support and supervise. The CEO and senior management team visit each school and meet with the entire faculty for a "Close the Loop" meeting every year to discuss the survey results and implications. This process underscores the priority this system places on using data to support improvement, and models the work we want teachers to do in improving their own practice.

There is a saying: "Every system is perfectly designed to get the results it gets."[9] If policy makers want to support teachers' professional growth and increase their effectiveness, then we need systems designed to deliver this result.

2

Ensuring Equitable Access to Great Teachers

FRAMING THE ISSUE

Kati Haycock and Sarah Almy

All students pay a high price when they are subjected to ineffective teaching. But the highest price is paid by those who can least afford it. Low-income students and students of color often face the steepest learning challenges, yet they are disproportionately paired with the weakest teachers.

Systems for measuring teacher effectiveness in terms of impact on student achievement are just starting to emerge. In the absence of reliable data on teachers' impact on student learning, we look to available proxy measures to assess teacher quality, such as experience, or demonstrated competence in a given subject matter (whether the teacher is considered "in field" or "out of field").

Neither are perfect proxies. However, until better measures are widely available, these can provide us with important information, particularly regarding which kids are getting the strongest teachers. And on this question, the answer is clear. No matter how you look at it, poor students and students of color are getting shortchanged in their access to quality teachers.

Core academic classes in high-poverty schools are almost twice as likely to have an out-of-field teacher as counterpart classes in low-poverty schools.[1] First-year teachers are assigned to high-poverty schools at almost twice the rate that they are assigned to low-poverty schools. This is not just an issue between districts or between schools. Even within schools, the deck is often stacked against our neediest students. A recent study of within-school sorting found that low-income, black, and low-achieving students are all more likely to be assigned to novice teachers.[2]

In the few places where data on teachers' effectiveness is available, we continue to see disparities in assignments. High-poverty and high-minority schools have fewer of the most effective teachers and more of the least effective teachers.[3] In Los Angeles, for example, a low-income student is more than twice as likely to have a bottom-performing English language arts (ELA) teacher as is a higher-income peer. Latino and African American students in Los Angeles are two to three times more likely to have bottom-quartile teachers in math and ELA, respectively, than their white and Asian peers.[4]

In 2001, when lawmakers worked to reauthorize the Elementary and Secondary Education Act, they recognized the need to address the persistent issue of inequitable access to quality teachers. The law required that low-income and minority students not be taught disproportionately by inexperienced, uncertified or out-of-field teachers. It also asked states to define minimum requirements for teachers to be considered as "highly qualified" and then work to get all teachers to meet this standard.

Unfortunately, while the ideas behind these provisions were right, the implementation was terribly flawed. First, no one paid attention to the equity data—districts and states didn't collect, report, or act on the data, and the federal government didn't make them. Second, rather than use the highly qualified teacher requirement as an opportunity to raise standards for teachers just as they were raising standards for students, most states created vague definitions littered with loopholes that allowed almost all teachers to immediately meet the definition, and that bypassed any opportunity to boost the quality of the teaching force. As a result, we now have systems that identify 95 percent of teachers as highly qualified; and because virtually all are highly qualified, we pretend that we have narrowed or eliminated quality gaps between high- and low-poverty schools.

The truth, however, is different—and most teachers know it. In far too many places, we *still* don't know who our best teachers are, let alone whether they are teaching the students who need them most. When we pretend that everyone is the same, we disadvantage our low-income and minority students, who are assigned weaker teachers year after year. We demoralize those effective teachers who receive no more recognition or increased responsibility than their less effective colleagues down the hall. And we limit the entire profession by failing to learn from our strongest teachers and to provide adequate and focused support to our weaker ones.

Thankfully, some districts and states are starting to recognize and address flawed systems for measuring teacher effectiveness. Yet just identifying good teachers will not guarantee that high-poverty and low performing schools will magically get more of them. Few places are actively focused on how to strategically address the conditions that attract and retain top teacher talent in high-poverty and low performing schools.

What would it take to get our best teachers in classrooms with the students who need them most—those whose futures would be so much brighter as a result? What could district, state, and federal policy makers do to make a difference?

MOVING THE WHOLE SCHOOL FORWARD

Talented Teachers for Turnaround Schools

Erin Dukeshire and Lisa Goncalves Lavin

We are teacher leaders in the Boston Public Schools. After seven and five years, respectively, in classrooms, we both felt frustrated with our roles, yet were committed to staying in the classroom. Our previous work showed that we were effective teachers, but we still wanted to grow professionally. And we wanted to do so as leaders within high-need schools, without leaving the classroom, where we could simultaneously effect change and grow our careers.

We were drawn to the dual challenges presented by leading change as teachers in turnaround schools: to teach low-income, high-need students—exactly the students who most need experienced, highly effective teachers—and also to take on leadership roles to effect schoolwide change. We were also drawn to the opportunity for increased compensation for our time and skills. We chose to apply to Teach Plus's Turnaround Teacher Teams (T3) Initiative because of the opportunity to collaborate with other thoughtful and committed teachers who were selected for the leadership cohort (see case study 2.1). The cohort model would allow us to be part of the problem-solving team to "turn around" a school and would afford us the opportunity to work with a team of people who were effective, informed, and dedicated, as proven through their past teaching experience. Most important, our fellow teacher leaders would share our belief that all children can succeed under the right circumstances, and together we would be part of strengthening the quality of teaching in high-need schools.

THE TURNAROUND MODEL

In the spring of 2010, the Blackstone Elementary School (where Lisa taught at the time) and Orchard Gardens K–8 Pilot School (where Erin currently teaches) were two of the thirty-five schools in Massachusetts designated "turnaround schools" by the state. Both schools' student test scores were consistently in the bottom 5 percent of schools statewide. The new state law required that turnaround schools begin with at least 50 percent new staff, and it granted the new principals, Dr. Steve Zrike and Mr. Andrew

Bott, flexibility to hand-select personnel. We each joined our schools as part of those new faculties.

Both principals set forth school redesign priorities with the belief that doing a few things deeply and consistently would produce rapid gains in students' learning. Today, in both our schools, teachers systematically collect and analyze student data to inform targeted instruction and interventions. Our schools also prioritize collaboration among people who are committed to the students' success—teachers, community partners, and families. By working together, we engage students and families to improve attendance and support learning at school and at home. Finally, our schedules devote additional time to students' learning and to adults' collaboration and professional development. Both schools have an extra hour of academic classes each day and partner with organizations that provide afterschool programs. Additionally, teachers' schedules include at least 130 extra hours of professional development and team meeting time, both during and outside of school time. The intensive work of the turnaround and fostering a professional learning environment are not things administrators can do on their own. This is where teacher leadership comes in.

TEACHER LEADERSHIP: WHAT WE DO

What does teacher leadership look like for us? We are classroom teachers who belong both to a school-based cohort of teacher leaders and a larger cohort of T3 Initiative teacher leaders across multiple schools. First and foremost, we are full-time classroom teachers. Our top priority is maximizing the achievement of the students in front of us every single day. Just like every other teacher in our buildings, we plan and deliver daily lessons, grade student work, build relationships with students and families, and attend weekly professional development sessions.

But we are also tasked with leading school-level change beyond our classrooms. Our teacher leader teams make up approximately 25 percent of all teachers at each of our schools. Instead of launching our year by preparing our classrooms and curricula as we did in our previous schools, now we attend an intensive summer institute with our full T3 Initiative teacher leader cohort, comprising teacher leaders from multiple schools, and all of our school administrators. This summer institute begins with professional development, which zooms in on leadership skills, but the

CASE STUDY 2.1

THE POWER OF TEACHER-LED SCHOOL CHANGE

The Turnaround Teacher Teams (T3) Initiative was designed as a way to solve a pernicious problem: staffing so-called hard-to-staff schools with experienced, effective teachers. In 2008, a group of thoughtful Boston teachers—the inaugural cohort of Teach Plus Teaching Policy Fellows—were challenging the dual assumptions that good teachers will not go to chronically underperforming schools and that poor kids can't learn.

These teachers honed in on five conditions that they believed would be necessary to attract outstanding, experienced teachers to work in struggling schools and lead efforts to turn those schools around:

- A guarantee of working with a sizable cohort of like-minded teachers who would be qualified both in the classroom and as peer leaders. Today T3 teacher leaders comprise 20 to 25 percent of each partner school's faculty, depending on school size.
- A rigorous selection process designed to be a fair and comprehensive way of assessing a teacher's readiness to be a turnaround leader.
- A defined leadership role that facilitates and supports the work of all teachers in the school to significantly increase student achievement.
- A strong, experienced principal who supports and empowers teachers and who values teacher leadership.
- Compensation for the additional time required to serve in their leadership roles through a salary differential that acknowledges their status.

Boston Public Schools, led by then Superintendent Carol R. Johnson, agreed to collaborate with Teach Plus to launch the T3 Initiative in 2009. In an overwhelmingly clear statement of belief in children, in teaching, and in the power of changing lives, qualified master teachers applied five deep for every available position in the first year of T3's existence in Boston. This trend has continued in successive years and in successive districts, hopefully putting to rest the assumption that great teachers will not go to low performing schools. Today, the T3 Initiative, led by National Director Meghan O'Keefe, operates in Boston Public Schools (BPS), Fall River Public Schools (Fall River, Massachusetts), and District of Columbia Public Schools.

The teachers chosen as T3 teacher leaders have, on average, nine years of experience. They have track records of success with urban students and arrive on their interview days with portfolios jammed with examples of how they use data and student work to guide their instruction. They are enthusiastic collaborators and humble, reflective practitioners. And they do not, for any reason, give up on children.

Why do these experienced teachers leave their current schools for schools with long track records of low achievement? They want to be teachers and leaders in schools focused on turning around. They want to be part of collaborative, solutions-oriented professional school cultures. And finally, they want the chance to work with strong, experienced school leaders and with like-minded colleagues.

SUPPORT FOR T3 TEACHER LEADERS

The T3 Initiative has invested heavily in support and development for T3 teacher leaders. This high level of embedded professional learning and support is what allows great teachers to take on this degree of additional responsibility—along with a full teaching load—and be successful at both.

This support wraps around T3 teacher leaders in the following ways:

- *Summer Institute:* Each school year starts with the entire cohort of T3 teacher leaders across schools coming together for intensive training focused on data analysis, the teacher-leader inquiry process, and the role of the teacher leader as a school's culture change agent.
- *School-Based Coaches:* These full-time coaches are embedded in every T3 partner school to support the weekly planning and growth of T3 teacher leaders and to plan relevant schoolwide and networkwide professional development.
- *Cross-Network Learning:* T3 coaches collaborate to set up cross-school learning opportunities so that T3 teacher leaders can learn from each other's best practices.

THE RESULTS

Data from the first two cohorts of T3 partner schools in Boston show that students in these schools are growing in English language arts and math at a faster pace than their peers in other Boston Public Schools and other Massachusetts turnaround schools. In just two years, students in T3 partner schools have nearly closed the English language arts achievement gap with students in the rest of BPS and other Massachusetts turnaround schools. In math, they have completely closed that achievement gap and continue to grow.

—Monique Burns Thompson

majority of our time is left to our individual school teams to analyze student data and build action plans. The summer institute also allows us to form relationships with other teacher leaders both within our schools and across schools so that we can share ideas and strategies that pertain to our leadership roles.

Then our school year begins. The numbers we analyzed over the summer become faces in front of us, each with his or her own personality and individual story. Our first weeks are devoted to getting to know the students, creating community within the classroom, and establishing routines and expectations.

Throughout the year, our first priority continues to be our students, but our attention is on not just advancing the learning of the students in our own classes, but also moving the whole school forward. When the first bell rings on Monday, we've already planned for the week ahead. The students arrive, and we work directly with them for four hours, combining whole group, small group, and individual instruction. By 11:00 a.m., we take our first deep breath and run to meet with our leadership coaches and teacher leader colleagues to plan our week's grade-level or content team meetings. Together, we reflect on our teams' progress and look ahead to the upcoming weeks. This allows us to plan and develop an agenda for the week's team meeting. The leadership coach often provides feedback on the agenda, suggesting facilitation approaches that will help the team to be most successful. On the way out of the meeting, we make a few quick copies for future lessons, stop at our mailboxes, and check school e-mail. Questions flood our minds: *Do I e-mail my team? Call Justin's family about his reading progress? Fill out the pile of student evaluations on my desk? Are there data or materials I need to gather for the team? Do I eat lunch?* We are constantly trying to balance supporting our teams with meeting the needs of the students, who deserve our complete attention.

With the return of our students to the classroom, we come back to the work of teaching for the next few hours. Knowing today that our teams will be analyzing current student data tomorrow, we carefully planned to wrap up our instruction and gather information on students' understanding before the end of the afternoon's classes. Yet, there are emotional and social conditions that we, as teachers, cannot always anticipate in our classrooms and that require our attention. Maria may have an outburst that disrupts her own learning, and the effects ripple through class.

Students may not understand the lesson as we designed it. We think on our feet, making rapid adjustments to serve our students' needs and to fulfill the commitments we've made to our teams. Between planning, engaging, caring for students, and being responsible for the team's work, we feel emotionally exhausted by the end of the students' day.

But our days are far from over. As students leave, we finalize lessons for the next day. Our phones buzz, alerting us of the time we've scheduled to work on other teacher leader responsibilities. Lisa meets with the family engagement and community outreach administrator to discuss, plan, and execute the afterschool program's current initiatives. Erin leads a summer academic program as part of her teacher leadership role. At times her community partners come to the school to plan the summer learning program on their end; other times, Erin speaks with teachers and parents to determine which students would benefit most from this summer experience.

By early evening, we pack our bags, tidy up our classrooms for the next day, and begin to consider what other work needs to get done this evening.

SCHOOL-BASED TEACHER LEADER TEAMS

The alarm rings the next day, and we ready ourselves for our first several hours of teaching. By midmorning we are on our way to facilitate our team meetings. Each teacher brings updates from other school leadership teams, their own classrooms, and from our community partners. Next, we look at our students' data to celebrate their successes and identify struggles. Working together, we share teaching strategies and fine-tune instruction to improve the students' areas of weakness. The rest of the meeting is spent collaboratively planning, looking at student work, creating or finding appropriate assessments, and planning family events or science fairs. At these meetings, we facilitate teachers. Our job is to ensure that all team members have their voices heard, and that all teachers leave feeling that they are better prepared to serve their students.

As teacher leaders, we have many opportunities to facilitate meetings with our colleagues. In addition to leading grade-level or content teams, teacher leaders plan and facilitate meetings of the Instructional Leadership Team (ILT) every two weeks. This is a proactive advisory body open to all interested teachers and administrators for discussion of issues related to teaching, learning, assessment, and professional development.

Across our cohort of T3 Initiative partner schools, we also visit other teacher leaders' schools to learn more from each other. When Orchard Gardens' teachers visited the Blackstone, first-grade teachers at the Blackstone shared how they departmentalize their first-grade students. Two teachers are responsible for teaching math, and two teachers are responsible for teaching writing. The writing and math blocks are heterogeneously grouped so that the English language learners are exposed to peers with fluent English. The first-grade teachers at the Blackstone see this as an effective model, as students are getting authentic language practice and teachers are able to plan and refine lessons devoted to just one content area. Moreover, the students' assessments have shown tremendous growth. To be able to integrate students heterogeneously by their language needs and teachers in this way requires a deep sense of trust and commitment. Having these conversations across school sites allows teacher leaders opportunities to engage with different ideas and perspectives, and to observe effective teaching methods to take back to their own schools.

CONDITIONS FOR SUCCESS

We believe there are fundamental conditions that must be in place for teacher leaders to succeed.

Shared Leadership and Trust

Our teacher leader roles are rooted in our administrators' shared belief that school turnaround is too big a job for one leader. Steve Zrike, now the former principal at the Blackstone, believes deeply that "sustained and deep-rooted school turnaround requires that a critical mass of passionate educators share and act on a collective responsibility to transform the educational experience for traditionally underserved children." Orchard Gardens principal Andrew Bott also embraces the idea of shared leadership and trust in collaboration. As Bott says, "Success comes when teams of teachers are empowered and trusted to make the decisions that are best for their students."

Furthermore, both administrators share a clear and informed vision of schools where all children could be successful. During Erin's interview with Bott, he explained that Orchard Gardens would not only succeed in improving achievement, but would become the best school in

Massachusetts. Since then, he has held that high bar for administrators, teachers, and students, and has held his vision constant. Both administrators communicate their vision to the staff by having an open-door policy and transparency about their decision making.

Structures That Support

Both our schools use research-based structures that support teacher leaders in facilitating teacher-driven decision making. These structures, such as common lenses for analyzing student data, allow teams to have a shared language but also the independence to make decisions that are best for their students. Therefore, all team decisions are data based, with the goal of answering the questions: "Is this what our student(s) need? Is this our best teaching leverage point?" Focusing on data builds trust among members of a teacher team so teachers can work together to determine the best moves for increasing student progress. Teachers do not have to wonder if a colleague simply doesn't like their teaching methods. They know decisions will be made on objective, concrete assessment results. Using data in a cycle of teaching, assessing, and reteaching builds trust and invests teachers to learn from one another. Teachers are genuinely interested in learning their colleagues' approaches to teaching a certain skill set, asking each other, "How do you teach this?" Finally, data measures give us both a shared way to communicate about students and a shared accountability for all students in the teams.

Making data-based decisions requires that time be set aside for teachers to collaboratively analyze data. Both our administrators value and protect this time for teachers to meet in teams. Class schedules are built around the need for each teacher team to meet for ninety uninterrupted minutes every week. Meeting time is treated the same as teaching time; it cannot be interrupted to ask a teacher to do other tasks.

High Expectations and Feedback

While we both feel supported and trusted by our administrators, we are aware of their high expectations of us, and we strive to meet them. In the interview process to become teacher leaders, we had to exhibit data showing our past students' gains and our knowledge of pedagogy and content areas. Knowing that we were effective teachers to begin with, our principals held high expectations of us from the start, but also identified areas where we could continue to grow.

Authentic and specific feedback communicates administrators' high expectations for teachers and students. For instance, Lisa can still remember one of Zrike's first suggestions. Being in a school with 53 percent of students learning English as a second language, Zrike often mentioned that students needed frequent opportunities to talk. Observing Lisa's classroom, he commented that all students should speak in complete sentences at all times if they are to be college bound. Upon reflection, Lisa noted that this high expectation was not one she had communicated to her students. She quickly made this adaptation in her classroom. Within two months, she was amazed (and still is) by the impact this had on her students' learning in speaking, reading, and writing. Clear, immediate, actionable, and high-impact feedback is not only important, it also conveys high expectations in a school with high stakes. Finally, it made Lisa want to achieve her highest potential, as it was clear to her that not only was she supported, but risk taking to improve instruction in her classroom was valued.

Specific and positive feedback builds our confidence to lead our teams. At the beginning of the turnaround, Erin was a timid facilitator of team meetings. Not knowing other teachers' approaches to instruction or whether her style fit with the school's goals, she would hesitate to propose her own ideas and would quickly back down when challenged. After her principal had made several visits to her classroom and provided Erin with specific, positive feedback, she felt confident that her teaching methodology aligned with the school vision. His suggestions for improvement also communicated to her the ways he expected teachers to grow in their practice. This helped her feel more comfortable proposing ideas to her team and better equipped to handle conflicting ideas without losing her vision for the team.

Quality of the Cohort

In addition to a supportive administration, the quality of the teacher leader cohort is key to making teacher leadership effective. In our leadership program, a rigorous interview process ensures that teacher leaders share the fundamental belief that all students can succeed and also have the skills needed to turn around student performance. Teacher leaders come to the program with an existing teaching skill set that allows them to see beyond their own classroom and students, and to focus on the needs of the school as a whole.

One of the skills that teachers bring to this leadership role is their proven ability to collect and analyze data in order to make instructional decisions for their students in all content areas. Before applying to be teacher leaders, we had clear content knowledge and knew how to communicate and guide our colleagues to have that same knowledge. In the collaborative team meetings, teams discuss data and think about appropriate teaching steps, and share ideas and/or strategies that they have used or seen used for student success. As teacher leaders, we found it challenging at first to facilitate data inquiry cycles with first-year teachers, who needed and valued the time for planning more than for data analysis. It took time and patience for the group to trust in the data inquiry cycle—to trust that looking at and acting on the data would result in real student gains. This process forced us to face resistance with a steadfast school goal in mind, so that the team could embrace shared accountability for our students as a grade-level team and not just in individual classrooms.

Willingness to Improve

The teacher leader cohort also needs to be willing to continuously improve its skill set as team facilitators. Our leadership roles bring challenges unlike those we have learned to overcome in our own classrooms. How would we lead teams of teachers who had been teaching longer than we had? How could we lead a data analysis meeting when our own students' test scores may have been lower than those of our colleagues? Erin, in particular, struggled with getting her team on board with a shared goal. The science team ranged from kindergarten through eighth-grade teachers, from first-year teachers to those with more than a decade of experience. Additionally, not all teachers were facing a standardized state test. She was equipped to meet the needs of diverse students, but did not have the same experience with adults.

From administrators designated to coach the teacher leaders, we learned to begin the year by writing team norms, delineating roles, and creating common goals. By collaborating with our wise colleagues in the cohort, we acquired new strategies for dealing with our teams' challenges. Leadership challenges and advice are exchanged openly at cohortwide meetings, but more often during informal hallway chats. Then, through trial and error, we implement ideas and find out what works. The teacher leaders are dedicated to learning how to get their teams running smoothly.

Importance of School Culture

Schools need to develop cultures where all teachers are comfortable with differentiated roles that build on their strengths or personal interests in education. In the beginning days of the turnaround, it appeared that the staff was unclear that some teachers would hold leadership roles, and they were unaware of how those teachers were selected. On Erin's first day at Orchard Gardens, another teacher whispered to her, "Hey, I don't know who the department chair is, but I nominate you to do it." Teachers she met were either unaware that their content teams would have a leader, or were unsure how a leader would be named when no veteran staff remained to fill the position. The effects of this during the early weeks of the turnaround process shook our confidence as team leaders and made it clear that trust and relationships needed to be formed before real teamwork could happen. Our administrators were eager to help in this. It is important that teacher leadership roles are formalized and clearly communicated across the school, but our administrators also make sure to publicly celebrate successes of teams, never suggesting that the success of a team is due to its leader alone.

For teacher leadership to be successful, administrators must hold the fundamental belief that all teachers are capable of leadership. They have to demonstrate the belief that they are seeking all teachers' ideas to move the work forward. During the first year of the turnaround, several teachers outside of the T3 Initiative cohort were asked to lead initiatives at Orchard Gardens that they felt strongly about. This belief that all teachers have the ability to fill leadership roles will also sustain success in the years following the turnaround initiative.

CONCLUSION

Teacher leadership roles attracted us to chronically underperforming schools. This work is tough, demanding, and exhilarating. The conditions for successful teacher leadership include a strong cohort of teachers, supportive administrators who believe in shared leadership, and fair compensation for the extra skills and responsibilities required of teacher leaders. After three years as teacher leaders, we are convinced that this model works—both to attract great teachers to struggling schools to improve those schools for students and to offer teachers an opportunity to learn and expand their impact beyond a single classroom. Students at schools with the T3 Initiative and other interventions in place are making greater progress than those at turnaround schools without formalized shared leadership.[5] In our classrooms, we see the impact on individual students. Lisa's students began the year speaking in two-word English phrases and left first grade speaking in complete sentences. They also fell in love with reading chapter books. Erin's students became true scientists, collecting data about the phases of matter and eagerly dissecting frogs.

Shared leadership can transform a school and transform the lives of our students. But sustaining this impact over time, and allowing teachers to do this work effectively while still serving the students in our individual classrooms, requires a whole-school commitment to both the vision and the allocation and protection of resources to make it happen. When schools make this commitment, we've seen that it can and does draw effective teachers to work in high-need school environments, and to stay in these classrooms that need them most.

EDUCATION LIBRARY
UNIVERSITY OF KENTUCKY

RESPONSE

Kati Haycock and Sarah Almy

In opening this chapter, we outlined the current landscape of access to qualified teachers around our country, illustrating that far too many of our most disadvantaged students are not getting their fair share of good teachers. We highlighted the inattention to this issue in policy at the federal and state levels. However, addressing issues of equitable access to effective teachers requires both policy action and on-the-ground efforts to improve in-school conditions for teaching and learning.

The work in Boston that Erin Dukeshire and Lisa Goncalves Lavin highlight is a promising example of what can happen when smart policy and thoughtful practice combine to create opportunities for good teachers to move to and stay at struggling schools. On the policy side, Massachusetts' requirements for turnaround schools brought new talent into long-failing schools and freed the hands of school leaders to make smart and strategic staffing and management decisions. And on the practice side, Boston Public Schools and Teach Plus seized upon the new policy to launch the T3 Initiative, which is designed around recruiting and keeping a concentration of top talent in the highest-need schools.

Sometimes policy makers and others hear the words "equitable access to effective teachers" and assume that the only way to achieve this is to move teachers around like pawns in order to create an even distribution. However, to be clear—forced assignment is *not* a smart solution to issues of inequitable access. Instead, to correct systemic flaws, we must address policy and culture issues that prevent schools serving large populations of low-income students and students of color from getting and keeping high numbers of effective teachers.

When district leaders actually stop to ask strong teachers what would convince them to teach where they are most needed, their answers, as Dukeshire and Lavin demonstrate, are clear and unequivocal: they want a strong leader who cares a lot about quality instruction; a collaborative, mission-focused working environment; opportunities for ongoing development and support; and they want to teach with other strong teachers. Despite common perceptions to the contrary, it turns out that there are lots of strong teachers who really do want to teach the kids who most need them. But it takes more than just incentive pay or a pat on the head to get and keep them there.

Research has found that the work environment in schools matters more to teacher satisfaction and retention than do the demographics of the students in the school.[6] There are a few conditions that are especially important to teachers; these align closely with those that Dukeshire and Lavin identify as critically important to teacher leader success. One such condition is effective school leadership, which includes maintaining high expectations for all students and staff, creating a positive school culture centered on a shared vision, and developing structures to support staff and provide them with ongoing feedback and opportunities for professional growth (the importance of great school leadership is addressed more broadly in chapter 6). Another crucial condition is a sense of staff cohesion, including regular chances to collaborate with colleagues and a sense of shared accountability for the students in the building. Both these factors are very present in Dukeshire's and Lavin's descriptions of their schools, so it is no surprise that these are great places for strong teacher leaders to grow and thrive.

Dukeshire and Lavin also emphasize the importance of shared leadership models, and we couldn't agree more that models such as the ones they describe should be more common in all of our schools, and particularly in our highest-need schools. In the coming years, more and more schools will roll out challenging college- and career-ready standards and rigorous systems for measuring teacher performance and supporting teacher development. With these new demands, even very strong principals must figure out how to effectively share responsibilities in order to leverage talent within their buildings and add capacity to accomplish the work that must be done.

The gathering movement toward evaluating teacher performance marks an important step forward in the ongoing effort to strengthen our nation's schools. If current efforts to identify effective teachers are to make a difference for students, however, they must go beyond merely identifying these teachers. In almost all cases, these efforts currently fail to ensure that new information about teacher performance and teacher quality is actually used to identify and act on issues of inequitable student access to effective teachers.

Done right, improved teacher evaluation and support systems, in coordination with attention to equitable access to effective teaching for all students, could be tremendously powerful in helping to eliminate persistent gaps in achievement. With information on how effective teachers are growing student learning, districts could be more deliberate and strategic about creating conditions that attract, grow, and keep strong teachers in the most disadvantaged schools. But this change will not occur on its own. Federal and state policy must prioritize attention to this issue. And then, as illustrated so nicely by these teacher leaders, districts and schools must act to remove barriers and create conditions that ensure our neediest students have access to great teachers.

3

Measuring Teacher Effectiveness

FRAMING THE ISSUE

Jason Kamras

As every parent—and every child—knows, teachers are not all the same. The best in the profession make learning come alive, inspire their students to achieve at the highest levels, open young minds to new ways of thinking, and bring joy and love to their classrooms each and every day. But other educators struggle with even the basics.

Because of this variation in teacher performance, parents around the nation do everything they can to get their children into the best teachers' classrooms, and they work with equal passion to avoid those educators who are known to be less effective.

At the same time, our public policy treats teachers as interchangeable "widgets," to use the term popularized by TNTP's insightful study on this subject.[1] For example, in almost every school system in America, a teacher's compensation has absolutely nothing to do with performance. In fact, a mediocre teacher could be making much more money than an outstanding one if he or she has more years in the system or has an advanced degree. The widget effect also plays out when budget-based layoffs are necessary. In most districts, the newest teachers, not the lowest performing ones, are let go first. And most troubling of all, in 2008, when we started to build IMPACT, District of Columbia Public Schools' rigorous, multiple-measure evaluation tool, very few school systems had evaluation systems that would even allow them to make performance-based decisions about their teachers. While many districts and states are now in the process of building better evaluation systems for their teachers, effective implementation of those systems—and effective use of the data they will provide—remain a work in progress.

The widget effect is most alarming because a vast body of research tells us that great teachers—unlike their lower performing colleagues—have a profoundly positive effect on the children they serve. As Eric Hanushek of Stanford University notes: "Three years of good teachers (eighty-fifth percentile) in a row would overcome the average achievement deficit between low-income kids (those on free or reduced-price lunch) and others."[2] Put simply, great teachers close the achievement gap. And the reverse is also true: low performing teachers maintain or actually widen the gap.

Failing to pay attention to performance hurts not only children, but also teachers. No high performing individual—whether he or she works in education, law, medicine, engineering, business, journalism, or any other profession—wants to work with low performers. Thus, the path to truly great schools, and a truly professional teaching force, is not blindness to effectiveness, but rather a laserlike focus on it.

This insight has energized a movement of education reformers who believe in making effectiveness the driver of all policy decisions related to a teacher's career, from recruitment to professional development to compensation. Essential to this effort is the creation of robust teacher evaluation systems that will enable district leaders to make strategic, performance-based decisions about their teachers.

But defining exactly what makes a teacher great, and what he or she should be held accountable for, is a complex matter. What do you think teachers should be held accountable for? What role should student achievement play? Should anyone other than principals participate in the evaluation process? How can we capture all the intangible contributions that great teachers make? What would make an evaluation system fair *and* rigorous?

SATISFACTORY? ME?

Giving New Teachers the Support They Deserve

Stephanie Widmer

I walked into my first evaluation meeting five years ago eager and ready to learn. I didn't know much about what to expect—my assistant principal had observed me a few weeks before, and I couldn't wait to hear what she had to say about my classroom. I was desperate for feedback. She'd seen me working with my sixth graders on a tough skill—creating outlines for our expository papers. I figured she'd have a lot to share. After all, I was a first-year teacher, and I knew I had a ton of room to grow.

At the meeting, my AP laughed, gave me a pat on the back for making it that far into the school year, and to my honest-to-goodness surprise, signed off on a satisfactory rating. How could that be possible? I'd just started teaching. Research shows that I'm not alone in this experience of evaluation: just a few years ago, before the rollout of many states' new evaluation tools, TNTP found that less than one percent of teachers received unsatisfactory ratings.[3] And a national survey of teachers, conducted in 2012 by Teach Plus, found that nearly half of all teachers surveyed had either not had an evaluation in the past year, or had not found their evaluation feedback useful.[4] Needless to say, my first evaluation taught me little to nothing about my teaching, but I did learn a lot about who would be coaching me to further develop my practice at this school—I would.

Several years later, at a different school with a much more rigorous evaluation system in place, I found myself walking into my first evaluation meeting, again, eager and ready to learn. My principal had already observed me at least ten times in short spurts over the course of the year, and I couldn't wait to hear what she had to say about my classroom. I was desperate for feedback. After all, I was a fourth-year teacher, and I had a ton of room to grow.

This evaluation meeting couldn't have been more different from the first one. My principal walked me through quotes she had recorded from me, examples from my students, and evidence from my planning. She explained her ratings to me. Yes, in some categories, I was meeting or exceeding expectations, but we also pinpointed areas for growth. In order to improve my minilessons in reader's and writer's workshop, we picked a book for me to read, fellow teachers to observe, and a template I could use for future lessons. With those targeted areas determined, my principal and I came up with clear next steps. Instead of having to coach myself, I now have a trusted partner on whom I consistently rely to help me be a better teacher for my students.

The regular, ongoing feedback I get from my principal also increases the trust I have in the formal evaluation process. I really believe that trust is something you build, and each interaction in which my principal and I discuss my growth, even in a quick conversation in the hallway, adds to that. I trust the formal evaluation process because of the level of dialogue about my work that she and I have had by the time it comes around.

My first school, it may seem, placed little to no value on teacher evaluations. But there is, of course, context to that. My Los Angeles Unified School District (LAUSD) campus served over 1,900 students with over 80 teachers. There were only four administrators. My current charter school serves just over 500 students with about 20 teachers. There are still four administrators. Of course my current principal is able to give me serious time and evaluation—our school is built to support a principal-as-coach model, and our students do very well because of this priority. I don't think my former school was disinterested in helping teachers improve, but our administrators' time was so consumed with keeping 2,000-plus people safe and contained that I can see now why evaluation wasn't a priority—it simply wasn't feasible.

Looking at the rigorousness of the teacher evaluation process at a school campus or within a charter organization can give us insight into the value that it seems to place on the process, but I think it also reflects greater issues at work. How do we staff schools? What is the vision for an administrator's role? Do we want to grow our teachers? Or do we simply want to keep them in the classroom?

My current school gives me much hope about what is possible not only for students, but also for teachers. I want all teachers and students to be in institutions where teachers are coached constantly. I get feedback from my principal and my peers inside and outside of the formal evaluation process. My door is literally always open, and teachers pop in constantly. I've also invited my colleagues to bring their classes in to observe our debates and writing celebrations. This serves as an exciting preview of eighth grade for younger students, but I also know that I'll get strong feedback from the teachers who bring their classes to my room. My development feels like an ongoing conversation rather than something I could have missed if I had blinked.

What will we have to change at schools in order to make this kind of ongoing development possible on a larger scale? A school like my first one, with so many teachers and so few administrators, should perhaps consider freeing up some of their more experienced, effective teachers' time to observe and provide feedback to beginning or struggling teachers. This could take some of the pressure off administrators and deepen the knowledge and skill set of those teachers at the same time.

Even where this isn't feasible, there are ways to make observations more meaningful at large institutions like my first school. After all, my assistant principal did make time to observe me; it's just that the feedback itself was not at all helpful. If she had been able to use a more detailed rubric, or if we had met before the observation so that I could highlight the kind of feedback I was looking for, that same classroom visit could have impacted my teaching much more than it did. Regular, detailed observations and meetings may present challenges in larger schools with limited resources, but there are ways to work within such limitations and still provide actionable feedback to teachers.

While I don't yet have all the answers, I do know that we absolutely must give our teachers the time and space to get meaningful feedback from their reviewers in order for evaluations to truly improve teachers' practice. Without that time and space, teachers won't be getting much from their evaluations—meaning that students won't be getting much from them, either.

HIGH IMPACT

It's the Feedback That Adds Value

Dwight Davis

My initial years of teaching were excruciatingly difficult. One might think that the most difficult skill to master for a new fifth-grade teacher within the District of Columbia Public Schools (DCPS) would be behavior management. Not for me. I was 6'6" and weighed 235 pounds. I'd played semiprofessional basketball in the United States and abroad—one look from me and my class was in line. I didn't have a lot of difficulty managing student behaviors. What proved to be most challenging during those initial years was managing the curriculum in such a way that all students were engaged and, most important, invested.

In particular, it was a challenge for me to bring all the threads of the curriculum together successfully to make my classroom an engaging place for learning. As the school year progressed, my students and I (and many of my students' parents, too) began to figure things out. Students submitted more homework, reading became more exciting, and I began to understand how to successfully design my reading and math blocks. But despite my successes, I continued to feel defeated. I spent most nights scripting lessons and doing research in preparation for the next day's instruction. My weekends were no different. I had no idea of the vastness of the education system beyond my unit plans and learning stations. I had no idea where or how to seek the help I needed to improve my practice as a teacher. But DCPS's new evaluation system, IMPACT, changed this for me. The feedback that IMPACT provided was the final ingredient I needed in order to see how all the elements of my classroom practice could fit together and boost my students' engagement and achievement.

Before IMPACT, our evaluation system was a bit of a mystery. I didn't know when observations would take place, how feedback would be shared, or, most important, the criteria by which I would be evaluated. My mission was clear: I was expected to seek out new teaching strategies and raise my students' achievement levels. But I didn't have much help getting there.

When IMPACT was introduced, some teachers and principals viewed it as a mechanism that would rid the system of low performing teachers; others saw it as a means to reward high performing teachers. Still others saw IMPACT as an essential cog in the wheel of education reform. But though it is an imperfect system, I have found IMPACT to be essential to my development as an urban educator.

Much of the discussion about (and pushback to) IMPACT has concerned the infamous Individual Value Added (IVA)—the component of a teacher's evaluation based on student test scores, which was initially set at 50 percent of the overall evaluation and has since been revised to 35 percent. But the perhaps less-acknowledged but more critical piece of IMPACT is that it also introduced a new way for teachers and their evaluators to interact and communicate. Where the previous evaluation system was seemingly based on the evaluator's subjective perceptions of the classroom environment and/or lesson, the language of evaluations under IMPACT is nestled within something called the Teaching and Learning

Framework (TLF). The TLF is a rubric that is used by independent evaluators (former expert teachers known as master educators) and administrators to frame their formal and informal evaluations.

The TLF has provided my evaluators and me with a common language and common standards for teaching and learning that enable me to target specific areas of my practice for growth. If a master educator visits my classroom and gives me a low mark on my ability to maximize instruction time, she can then provide me with resources and strategies to help me improve in this particular area. This wasn't the norm before IMPACT. Now I have a mechanism by which my practice is constantly being refined.

In this way, IMPACT has empowered me to seek out help. It has provided me with the language and tools to ask for specific help in a particular area where I may be weak. Whether that guidance comes from my colleagues, administrators, or master educators, when I ask for help under a specific standard of the TLF, the people around me know exactly how to assist me and which tool to provide me with. One such tool, for example, is Reality PD, a new professional development tool DCPS launched that consists of online videos to help teachers improve their practice. Using this tool is very simple. After identifying the standard in need of improvement, I am able to watch videos of how my highly effective colleagues perform in this area. In many instances, watching these videos is just as instructive as speaking with an administrator or a master educator.

IMPACT has also increased teacher collaboration within my school and across the district. Over the past four years, I have developed relationships with my master educators and even stronger bonds with the teachers within my school. My colleagues, often unprompted, forward me articles in the areas in which I have asked for help. I regularly speak with and observe other teachers within my school, especially those who have been rated "highly effective," in an effort to hone my practice and help others develop theirs. There are even opportunities for teachers to visit other classrooms across the district to improve DCPS's overall quality of teaching.

Of course, the usefulness of IMPACT's Teaching and Learning Framework should not be considered entirely distinct from IMPACT's student test scores component. When IMPACT was initially introduced, this was the aspect of our new evaluation system that troubled me most: the inclusion of student test data as a means of assessing my effectiveness. With so many extraneous variables affecting the lives of the students and families

I serve, I thought, "How could such a measure be fair?" But I have found that there is strong correlation between my TLF rating and my IVA scores. My focus on the TLF rubric, my collaboration with colleagues and master educators, and my work to improve in areas of need have resulted in academic success for my students. Don't get me wrong: there have been instances when my efforts did not yield the score I thought my students or I deserved. But in those instances, I have learned something very valuable about my practice. Whether it was to embed more test preparation strategies within instruction or focus more on small group instruction, I have been able to make the necessary adjustments to help the next class of students improve. To this end, IMPACT has provided a means for teachers to get the feedback we need to improve. And as the TLF rubric has enabled me to better drive instruction within my classroom, that greater efficacy has improved my students' performance on summative assessments, too.

My goal has always been to be a highly effective educator within DCPS. The students, parents, and communities that I serve deserve nothing less. However, achieving such a score requires an unrelenting desire to be prepared, innumerable hours of planning, constant data analysis, and a commitment to improving. No one ever said raising achievement in this urban vastness we call DCPS was easy. However, with IMPACT I feel that I am being equipped with the tools necessary to close the achievement gap for my students.

Many of my students enter the classroom as reluctant learners. By year's end, after many afterschool tutoring sessions and close collaboration with parents, my students are engaged learners. IMPACT has taught me how to work smarter and improve my practice. As I have continued in this process, my evaluation scores have continued to improve. Needless to say, IMPACT is making me a better teacher—and my students are winning.

URGENCY BREEDS ANXIETY

The Challenge of Building Teacher Trust

Peter Tang

During my first year of teaching in Memphis, I had dinner with a highly regarded veteran history teacher—the kind of teacher we all think back to for the great learning moments in our lives, and the kind whom my own district now calls an "Irreplaceable."[5] But what I remember most about that dinner aren't the great strategies he shared or the crash course in the institutional history of our school, but rather the sheer anxiety and exhaustion on my mentor's face when we discussed teacher evaluation. He felt attacked by the process, and believed that the drive to evaluate was more a drive to terminate. He doubted that the support everyone claimed teachers would get would ever materialize. He doubted the use of one-off test scores as accurate measures of learning. He doubted the intentions of those who push so hard for these evaluations.

Frankly, who could blame him? For decades, evaluation has been little more than a checklist or a thumbs-up. Professional development systems for teachers across the country have lacked rigor and failed to offer differentiated learning opportunities. Why should this teacher, after so many years of the status quo, believe that this time things would be different? And worse, why is such an accomplished teacher anxious over a system that would likely recognize and praise him?

Whether or not the change in the approach to teacher evaluation proves to be different hinges on how it is rolled out. As a teacher striving to do my best for my students, I need little convincing that the more information I have about how I'm doing, the better I can perfect my craft. Memphis City Schools is leading the charge on helping teachers understand how they are doing.[6]

My district launched its Teacher Effectiveness Initiative, a program intended to develop policies that support great teaching, in 2010, and since then has been working on a new system for defining and measuring teacher effectiveness (the Teacher Effectiveness Measure, or TEM). To their credit, they've solicited feedback from teachers throughout the development process (see case study 3.1).

Districts across the country have followed Memphis's lead and are rapidly developing their own tools for measuring teacher quality. Indeed, this is perhaps the most urgent priority for departments of education across the country—an important acknowledgment that great teachers are instrumental in a great education system. Lost in all of this urgency, though, is careful attention to the effectiveness of current professional support for teachers, an acknowledgment of historical drags on teacher effectiveness, and a clear transitional period to allow teachers to buy in to new evaluation tools before they're used for high-stakes decisions. We have too much to gain from this teacher effectiveness work to allow a rushed attempt to turn promising work into yet another failed run at education reform.

CASE STUDY 3.1

THE ROLE OF TEACHER VOICE IN DEVELOPING MEMPHIS'S TEACHER EFFECTIVENESS MEASURE

BACKGROUND

In 2010, Memphis City Schools (MCS) embarked on an initiative to ensure that students across the city were being taught by terrific teachers. MCS established the Teacher Effectiveness Initiative (TEI) to design policies to support a strong teaching force. One goal of the TEI was to create a broad measure of teacher performance that could be used as a factor in employment decisions. The resulting Teacher Effectiveness Measure (TEM) comprises several components, including classroom observations, stakeholder feedback, assessments of teacher knowledge, and measures of student growth in the classroom.[1]

In building the TEM, MCS designed a process to solicit teacher and other stakeholder feedback. During the 2010–2011 school year, MCS tested three observation tools (or "rubrics") that evaluators could use to objectively evaluate teachers in their classrooms. They tested the rubrics in 500 classrooms. In addition, MCS conducted two districtwide surveys to solicit teacher feedback on evaluations.

COLLABORATION WITH TEACH PLUS

Teach Plus works to ensure that solutions-oriented teachers have a voice in the policies that affect their classrooms. MCS collaborated with Teach Plus to elicit teacher feedback for use in the design of the TEM.

Teach Plus sponsored several events on evaluation and invited all MCS teachers to attend. At one such event in October 2010, using Teach Plus's live polling technology, teachers expressed dissatisfaction with the old system and openness to a new one. Specifically, 71 percent of teachers at the event said the current evaluation system did not support and improve their teaching practice.[2] Teachers were optimistic that a new system could be useful to improvement.

Teachers also indicated that an improved evaluation system could elevate their profession, and that using data as a part of that system could be beneficial.

1. To read more about the TEI, please visit http://www.scsk12.org/uf/TalentManagement/.
2. Data collected at live Teach Plus Network event, Memphis, October 28, 2010, http://www.teachplus.org/uploads/Documents/1293725888_20101028MemphisEventData.pdf.

At a January 2011 event, 96 percent of the teachers present agreed that clear, measurable standards of effectiveness are critical for teaching to be recognized as a true profession.[3]

Following the piloting of the three teacher observation rubrics, Teach Plus conducted three focus groups to gather feedback from teachers and evaluators about the value of the rubrics and to make decisions about which observation tool to use. By a clear majority, teachers identified District of Columbia Public Schools' IMPACT as the best observation rubric, and overwhelmingly preferred to make classroom observations as consequential as possible—40 percent of the evaluation rather than 35 percent—with stakeholder perceptions and teacher knowledge composing 10 percent. Student growth was set to make up the other 50 percent of the evaluation.

RESULTS

Memphis City Schools adopted the Teacher Evaluation Working Group's recommendations as centerpieces of the TEM: it selected IMPACT as a basis for the classroom observation rubric (with some modifications for the local context), and it heavily weighted classroom observations. In addition, the Tennessee Board of Education unanimously approved the TEM and said that it could be used by districts across the state. Thanks to this work, MCS moved from a teacher evaluation system that offered only up-or-down ratings of "satisfactory" and "unsatisfactory" to a multidimensional teacher evaluation system with five ratings that range from "significantly above expectations" to "significantly below expectations." And any district in Tennessee—from the Mississippi River to the Appalachian Mountains—could follow suit.

With the TEM, the now unified Shelby County Schools will be better able to discover and share best practices and identify teachers who are most in need of increased support. The measure also indicates which teachers would make the best mentors or be eligible for other leadership roles.

The fact that MCS included teachers throughout the design process ensured that it would be more impactful than if teachers had been excluded. In addition, teacher involvement has helped to encourage essential teacher buy-in as the system is implemented.

—Heather Peske

3. Data collected at live Teach Plus Network event, Memphis, January 31, 2011, http://www.teachplus.org/uploads/1371132000_Teach%20Plus%20Network%20Event%20Summary%20Data.pdf.

Fortunately, there are ways to implement evaluation systems so that the information gathered allows teachers to improve. I teach middle school math at a school with, fortunately, a fairly comprehensive and responsive menu of supports for my professional growth. With occasional in-classroom coaching by administrators and lead teachers, out-of-school in-person training sessions, teacher collaboratives, and carefully selected Web-based learning tools, my colleagues and I improve our craft under the direction of our principal. Even so, my school has only the beginning of what a robust professional support system should look like—and we could do better. We still lack the capacity to do timely trainings that address immediate classroom issues, the autonomy to quickly send teachers to appropriate conferences, and the human resources to create quality learning opportunities targeted at our teachers. Too much of our current model is district based, dictated by administrators who may mean well but often lack a deep understanding of teachers' needs. Districts need to offer schools the tools and flexibility to develop their own teachers' skills. Given a strong instructional leader and the right learning opportunities, the vast majority of struggling teachers can grow.

Effective professional development that will help teachers improve also assumes that teachers *believe* in the need to raise the quality of their impact on students—in other words, teachers need to trust the measures of evaluation. Our current testing data is grossly inadequate for diagnosing whether or not (and what) students are learning. Research on evaluation, such as the Bill and Melinda Gates Foundation's three-year Measures of Effective Teaching project, which was conducted extensively in hundreds of Memphis schools, has highlighted the benefits of using a variety of types of assessment—open response, pre- and post-school-year assessments, and higher order cognitive tests, to name a few—in measuring learning outcomes.[7] Student surveys provide another possible source of reliable information. Even so, school districts across the country are all too often tying evaluations to student growth as measured by one-off, end-of-year multiple-choice examinations.

While we will never realize the perfect learning measure, districts need to be wary of drawing conclusions from evaluations based on limited testing information. The adoption of Common Core–based assessments in the coming years should alleviate some of these concerns, as these tests are designed to be more closely linked to the critical thinking skills that really matter for our students. Tying teacher performance to pre- and post-assessments will address serious learning measurement issues such as summer learning loss. All the while, districts should heed teachers' advice for difficult-to-measure learning, such as in the arts and physical education. In Memphis, for example, we've adopted teacher-created portfolio rubrics in the arts. Teachers will then have better measures of their impact, and therefore a fairer basis from which they are assessed. Regardless, teacher input in the process of implementing assessment tools is critical both to securing trust from teachers and, indeed, to allowing evaluation to have the greatest positive impact on student learning.

Beyond the execution challenges of comprehensive evaluation, a larger historical problem arises if we make teachers the primary subjects of reform, particularly if we do so without allowing teachers themselves to set the agenda. The national achievement gaps—both among socioeconomic groups within the country and those seen between U.S. students and those in other countries—did not happen overnight. For decades, expectations for teachers were low. Most teachers who could keep classrooms of thirty students in order were considered good. As we have recently realized, this is not enough to prepare our students to succeed. My best teaching day comes when I challenge my students to think, to engage in intellectual discussion, and to solve problems while interacting in a respectful but challenging classroom environment—a far cry from the quiet, orderly classroom that once would have been considered good enough. Just as with students, if we don't expect much of teachers, we will not get much back.

As districts move on with evaluation work, they must recognize this historical reality—particularly for our veteran teachers—by giving teachers a reasonable amount of time to adjust to higher expectations and to grow to meet them. Taking action too quickly or too severely in the early years only serves to make teachers take the brunt of the blame for our educational system's inadequacies.

To ease in, data from the first two years of the evaluation system's implementation should be used strictly for prescriptive purposes, guiding teachers' development and the improvement of professional support systems. This gives districts time to hear from teachers, administrators, and stakeholders about the details of evaluation implementation and to adjust course as necessary. In Memphis, we've gone through TEM 2.0 and are already working on TEM 3.0, with heavy input from teachers and administrators working together. Once many of the kinks are worked out, *then* we can start the accountability clock for those teachers who are deemed to need improvement. By starting from a supportive stance, districts will enable greater teacher trust. The heralded veteran from my first year was much less anxious once he saw his own evaluation results. Rolling out new teacher evaluation tools is certainly urgent work, but it must not come at the expense of our respect for teachers' daily work.

It is important that I walk into the classroom every day and give my students the best education possible. Memphis's cutting-edge evaluation system keeps me in a constant growth mindset; it helps struggling colleagues meet the needs of their students; and it opens up a lively and important dialogue between administrators and teachers. But as we move forward with this process in Memphis and nationwide, we must be careful that shifting evaluation tools do not force teachers into a defensive posture by holding us accountable for unrepresentative data or by leaving us without adequate supports as we seek to grow in our chosen profession. Obviously, teacher evaluation is only one piece of a very large puzzle, as we need to hold school and district leaders tangibly responsible for their decisions. If we rush into evaluation changes, states and districts risk alienating the teaching force while making strategic decisions based on incomplete information. But do this right, listening to teachers along the way, and teacher effectiveness work has the potential to be a revolutionary tool for advancing student learning.

RESPONSE

Jason Kamras

Stephanie Widmer, Dwight Davis, and Peter Tang highlight some of the school systems and charter networks that have already placed a stake in the ground on defining and measuring teacher effectiveness. In Davis's section, we got an in-depth look at his experience of the District of Columbia Public Schools' effort to transform our teacher evaluation system through IMPACT, a system that assesses teachers in four areas: student achievement, pedagogical expertise, collaboration, and professionalism.

Davis and Tang both point to the complexity of measuring student achievement in particular. From a design perspective, too, the student achievement piece has been by far the most complex of these areas to measure. After all, students start the year at different skill levels, and they all face different factors outside the classroom that affect how they learn. At its core, a value-added model is a way of dealing with these challenges. It helps us estimate the teacher's impact on student learning as opposed to the impact of other factors, such as students' prior skill levels, the resources they have at home, or any learning disabilities they may have. In short, value-added data help us understand what the teacher did, apart from everything else.

How does it work? First, given a teacher's students' previous year's scores and other relevant information, we calculate how they are likely to perform, on average, on our state test. We then compare that likely score with the students' actual average scores. Teachers with above-average value-added scores are those whose students' actual performance exceeds their likely performance. In other words, in these classrooms, teachers helped their students beat the odds.

In the nontested grades and subjects, we must use a different approach. In the DCPS, at the beginning of the school year, teachers who do not have individual value-added data choose student learning goals tied to achievement on assessments other than the state test. Principals have the final say on whether the goals are sufficiently rigorous.

Once districts and charter networks have established systems for fairly and rigorously measuring teacher effectiveness, possibilities for other innovations in how we pay and support teachers open up. Based on data from IMPACT, DCPS is now able to differentiate compensation, giving significant bonuses (up to $25,000) and base salary increases (up to $30,000) to our best teachers. As Davis importantly points out, we also now know exactly who needs help and what kind of help they need. This has enabled us to be much more strategic with our professional development. For example, our school-based instructional coaches now use IMPACT data to more efficiently prioritize and target support for the teachers in their schools. And finally, we now know which teachers are not adequately serving children and need to transition out of the profession.

Many other states and districts are beginning to do this work as well. Some are funded by the federal "Race to the Top" initiative, which placed significant emphasis on effectiveness-based "human capital" reforms.

As school systems and states embark on this groundbreaking work, it is imperative that we include teacher voice in the process. Tang, in particular, addresses the importance of teacher buy-in to new evaluation systems: if evaluation tools are to achieve their most important goal—improving the quality of teaching in our schools—teachers must trust both the measures themselves and the support they'll receive to improve in any areas identified as weaknesses. And as Widmer illustrates, it is critical that school cultures grow to approach evaluation as an ongoing, collaborative process between teachers and administrators. If teachers feel that they receive constant support to improve and are recognized for their strengths through regular feedback from both administrators and colleagues, they will be more likely to trust formal evaluation tools and view them as one piece of an ongoing cycle of professional growth. With better tools to identify teachers' areas of strength and weakness, school systems have the ability to provide teachers with the feedback and development tools they need to do their best work, to push the profession toward one that seeks and rewards excellence from its practitioners, and to ensure that all children have the quality teachers they need to succeed.

4

Building a Performance-Driven Profession

FRAMING THE ISSUE

Celine Coggins and Lindsay Sobel

The challenge of transforming teaching into a twenty-first-century profession that meets the needs of students can be boiled down to a central question: how can we transition the seniority-driven orientation of teaching to a performance-driven orientation?

Ground zero in debates over the role of performance relative to seniority is: *Who gets to retain a teaching position when reductions in force are inevitable?* "Last in, first out," or LIFO, was the dominant policy in most school systems across the country as the financial meltdown of 2008 began to make its negative impact felt across all sectors. This chapter examines the profound legal and ethical battles that have emerged from this starting point.

THE RESEARCH ON VARIATION IN TEACHER QUALITY

Over the past decade, volumes of research have demonstrated that there is significant variation in teacher performance, which has dramatic influence on the life chances of children.[1] Top teachers routinely help students learn one-and-a-half years' worth of content in a year, while the weakest essentially slow students' progress down to half a year of progress over the full year. That's the difference a great teacher makes.

Importantly, variation in teacher performance does not correlate closely with years of experience, except at the start of one's career. In teaching, beginners tend to enter with varying levels of basic proficiency at helping students learn. Almost all teachers become substantially better over the course of their first three to five years in the classroom. After those initial years, individual performance tends to plateau.

Indeed, according to a recent study, only 13 percent of the teachers laid off with LIFO reductions in force would have been laid off in a system based on teacher effectiveness.[2] In other words, quality-blind systems retain many less-effective teachers and lay off more-effective ones. In the Los Angeles Unified School District (LAUSD), layoffs in 2009 and 2010 resulted in the loss of around 2,700 teachers. Among the approximately 1,000 K–8 math and English teachers for whom test scores were available, some 190 ranked in the top fifth among their colleagues, and 400 teachers were in the top 40 percent.[3]

This research evokes important questions about the role of seniority. If a fifth-year teacher is having a greater impact on students than his twenty-year-veteran colleague, why should the teacher with more years in the classroom automatically be guaranteed a job next year? Won't firing legions of newer teachers decimate the future of the teaching force just as retirements are accelerating on the horizon? The demographic data on teachers shows the impact baby boomer retirements are having, and will continue to have, on the profession, and presents a practical imperative for challenging LIFO as the default staffing policy in schools. The data on teacher effectiveness, moreover, presents a moral imperative for doing so.

MASSIVE GENERATIONAL UPHEAVAL

The year 2012 was projected to be the apex of baby boomer retirements from teaching. We've reached a pivotal moment in the history of the teaching profession in America. For the past forty-plus years, baby boomers have composed the majority of the teaching force—a great many serving full, distinguished careers from the late 1960s through to the present.

Data now reveal that the new millennium has ushered in a new majority of teachers. Those with less than ten years' experience now constitute almost 53 percent of the teaching force in schools across the nation.[4] This incoming group has the potential to shape how we educate children for the next several decades. Yet it remains to be seen whether this demographic tipping point will catalyze a seismic shift in schools or go virtually unnoticed.

In a strictly democratic sense, as a group ascends into the majority, it would be expected to have greater influence, but there is good reason for concern that this will not happen in teaching. Schools operate as seniority-driven cultures. The rules (i.e., for who is dismissed first in a layoff process, who is first in line for certain leadership opportunities, who gets to teach classes deemed most desirable) are set up to most benefit those with the greatest longevity. The message to young teachers has been: Wait your turn—accept the system as it is and it will work for you in time. In other words, assimilate or leave. The net effect over the past couple of decades has been the loss of countless thousands of teachers who took their sense of urgency and impatience for change and left the classroom.

Why does this population shift matter? We know that in recent history the average duration of a teaching career has decreased, especially for those teaching in urban schools. We know that Generation Y teachers want to be recognized for their accomplishments with increasing levels of leadership and authority. If the work of teaching cannot be transformed to accommodate these expectations—to allow career growth and leadership for those still directly teaching students—it is likely that temporary teachers will become the permanent situation in urban schools.

What's at stake is the very proposition that teaching is professional work. How does the incoming generation of teachers propose to chart a course to a future in which the work of teaching holds value for both the general public and for teachers themselves?

FROM NEW TEACHER TO TEACHER ACTIVIST

What I Learned from "Mr. Miller"

Tina C. Ahlgren

In my inbox, I still have the first e-mail I ever received from Indianapolis Public Schools. At the time, I thought it was just a job offer. In reality, it was the beginning of a life-changing journey. I'd never had an interest in urban education, but—fresh out of DePauw University—I was eager to secure a position for the fall.

Though I was teaching in one of the lowest performing schools in the state, I found I enjoyed the challenges, and I quickly became deeply engrossed in the school community. I had a demonstrably successful first year teaching high school algebra. My quirky sense of humor was a hit with the kids in my classroom, and they began to open up to me both academically and emotionally. Beneath the numerous academic and social challenges, they had hopes and dreams that I wanted to make sure came true. To help me out, there was a core group of families and teachers who were committed to making sure the school was moving in the right direction. By spring, I was leading professional development sessions, and my classroom organization and management strategies were presented by the administration as a model to the rest of the staff. I was thriving in an environment that I had never expected to be in, and I could not have been more excited for my future in the school I loved.

Yet, as the end of the school year approached, I was abruptly called into my principal's office. Clearly upset, she presented me with a letter and asked me to sign it. The school population was projected to decline, and due to my recent hire date, I was the one who had to go.

I remember crying inconsolably in a colleague's classroom, trying to figure out my next step. He kept telling me that I was lucky to at least have a guarantee of a job somewhere in the system rather than having been terminated altogether. I found little consolation in that fact. The thought of all the progress I had made and relationships I had built being for naught was heartbreaking. That's when I knew for sure that, to me, this was far more than just a job.

Staffing placement dates came and went, with no new position for me. I was on my honeymoon when I received an exciting phone call. As registration began, my school's enrollment outpaced projections, and my department chair demanded that I be reinstated to my previous position. I ended up staying at the school for another six years.

While I was fortunate to find myself right back where I wanted to be, other talented teachers were not so lucky. It was the first of many times that I watched passionate and successful educators forced out the door, simply because of their start dates.

Quality-blind staffing decisions create a disastrous cycle for urban students. Each year, the newest teachers receive layoff notices. To cover their legal responsibilities in the face of declining enrollment, the district is forced to give pink slips to more staff than is truly necessary. Rather than wait and hope, many get jobs in more affluent districts. Other teachers leave the profession altogether. So when positions do open up, many top teachers have already moved on. The district is forced to once again hire inexperienced first-year teachers to fill its positions, and the cycle continues. Yet another level of instability is added to students' already tumultuous lives.

The insanity of it all really hit home the year that "Mr. Miller" (not his real name) was forcibly assigned to teach middle school science at my school. Mr. Miller was a veteran teacher who had repeatedly been bounced from school to school. No one wanted him, but no one was willing to do the substantial work necessary to terminate his employment. He didn't even attempt to teach, but instead made the students sit quietly with no work while he read the newspaper. When students attempted to interact with him, he would become hostile and send them out of the room. Mr. Miller refused to perform even basic duties such as taking attendance. He had numerous formal reprimands on his record for insubordination and verbal abuse of students. It was gut-wrenching to know that despite numerous reductions in force (RIFs) that eliminated positions in his subject area, he remained (earning $30,000 more than an early career teacher).

Mr. Miller is, of course, an extreme example. I have worked with many veteran teachers who are amazing educators and mentors. But at the end of the day, urban students suffer when we allow date of hire to be the *sole* factor in staffing decisions. Staffing decisions must take into account many factors, including effectiveness, contribution to the school community, and experience. It is important to give veteran teachers some protection and job security, but the weight given to years of service should be minimal.

Mr. Miller was placed at my school soon after I became a Teach Plus Teaching Policy Fellow. Prior to my involvement there, I might have stood idly by and complained to my colleagues to no effect. However, with a group of like-minded teachers to support my efforts, I was empowered to stand up for justice on behalf of my students. I was also fortunate to have had this galvanizing experience at a time when the education climate was ripe for change.

For the first time, the local teacher union's leadership was willing to concede that our LIFO system of staffing was in need of drastic revision.

CASE STUDY 4.1

THE IMPACT OF TEACHER ADVOCACY IN CHALLENGING QUALITY-BLIND STAFFING POLICIES

BACKGROUND

In 2009, Teach Plus Teaching Policy Fellows in Indianapolis—all current teachers—identified quality-blind staffing policies as a critical issue that was both preventing Indianapolis Public School students from receiving the best possible education and costing the district scores of potentially high performing early career teachers. Many of these teachers had themselves experienced multiple layoffs in the early years of their careers. They shared the frustration that their performance in the classroom was not taken into account along with their years in the classroom when those layoff decisions were made.

LOCAL IMPACT

These teachers' advocacy led to the formation of a task force on layoffs that included the district superintendent, the local teacher union president, and two Teach Plus Teaching Policy Fellows (as well as the executive director of Teach Plus Indianapolis). Ultimately the group's proposal was brought to the union for a vote, and a change to the Indianapolis Public Schools teachers' contract resulted. On April 5, 2010, the Indianapolis Education Association approved a contract amendment that added performance measures to layoff decision making for first- through fifth-year teachers. Teachers in years six and beyond were not affected by this policy change.

The modified provision saved the jobs of large numbers of high performing young teachers, but it applied only to teachers in the first five years of their careers. Over the following year, teachers in Indianapolis continued to advocate for a more wide-reaching policy change. Teach Plus Teaching Policy Fellows served on both the state superintendent's Education Reform Cabinet and the state Evaluation Cabinet. In addition, Teach Plus convened opportunities for larger groups of teachers to meet directly with state legislators.

STATE IMPACT

In 2011, Senate Bill 1, an omnibus teacher quality reform package, became law in Indiana. The new state law required that all layoff decisions be made in the best interests of students. It transformed teacher evaluation and licensure, added new teacher leadership roles in the evaluation process, and required that performance—rather than seniority—be the primary basis of teacher layoff decisions. Today, Indiana has made great strides in ensuring higher standards for the education of students across the state.

Teach Plus Teaching Policy Fellows and other teachers in Indiana played a key role in advancing the core reforms of Senate Bill 1. They published op-eds, gave testimony before the legislature, and held public events to draw attention to the issue. Also important, they demonstrated that many current teachers are in favor of moving their profession toward one that prioritizes performance, both to best serve children and to recognize and elevate teachers as highly skilled professionals. Ultimately, these teachers were responsible for pushing their state to pass legislation that puts the best interests of children first.

—Celine Coggins

Several schools were facing potential state takeovers that could cost the district over 200 teaching positions. My cohort of Teach Plus Teaching Policy Fellows worked closely with the Indianapolis Education Association to assist in the development of an RIF system that took performance into account (see case study 4.1).

While excited for our success in Indianapolis, I was acutely aware of similar struggles in schools across the state. When legislation was proposed that would make comparable changes for all Indiana public schools, I gave feedback to lawmakers who sponsored the legislation, helping to ensure that the language was in the best interests of both students and teachers. I testified in favor of the bill before the Indiana House Education Committee. Once the bill successfully emerged from committee, I lobbied my representatives in the state house and senate. In an attempt to clear up some widespread misconceptions, I also wrote a letter to the editor that was published in the *Indianapolis Star.* After over a year of tireless work by teachers, Indiana passed a major education reform law overhauling the layoff system and requiring the kind of teacher evaluation system that can reliably identify top performers. Without these changes, Indianapolis Public Schools and other districts in the state could have lost an entire generation of our newest teachers.

Since then, I have worked to ensure that the law is implemented fairly. I began a term on the Indiana Department of Education's Education Reform Cabinet. In this role, I served as an intermediary between my district and the state with regard to teacher comments and concerns as the new evaluation model was developed. I am assisting teachers with understanding and navigating the new system, and instructing teachers on how to document their progress with new online tools.

When I think back to that day eight years ago, when the e-mail offering me a position in the Indianapolis Public Schools first popped up in my inbox, I can't help but be amazed at how much I have changed. I never could have envisioned the path that lay ahead—my evolution from a nervous beginning teacher, to a passionate student advocate, to a vocal political activist. What started as a job has become my life, and I've never regretted it for a moment.

LEAVING CHERIE

One Teacher's Experience of Last In, First Out

Jeanette Marrone

"I think this is the most peaceful I've ever felt."

Those were certainly not *my* words as a fledgling second-year teacher at an overcrowded, year-round middle school in south Los Angeles—but it was gratifying to hear them from my student. Cherie was part of an afterschool art club I had started that year with the goal of adding enrichment and creativity to my inner-city students' lives. One afternoon, I played different styles of music for them and asked them to paint using colors and brushstrokes that expressed how the music made them feel. For Cherie, a moment of inner peace came with "Porcelain," by Moby. It was a joy to witness her and her classmates expressing themselves artistically. For a moment, I felt peaceful too, knowing my hard work was making a difference in my students' lives by not only improving their academic skills, but also providing opportunities for life-enriching moments like these.

But that moment of peace faded quickly when Cherie asked enthusiastically, "Ms. Marrone, are we having art club next year?" My throat tightened. Telling Cherie that we would not be able to continue our club together was one of the most difficult experiences I have had as a teacher. But as one of my school's newest teachers, I was among the first to be laid off when the economy declined, and there was nothing that I or even my principal could do about it.

The politics of the union and the district were above Cherie's head as a sixth grader, so I simply told her that I did not want to leave, but I had no choice. Even though my departure was not my choice, I felt like I was abandoning her. I wondered what she felt. When the new school year began just a few days later (due to the school's year-round calendar), I was not there and neither was the art club.

Los Angeles Unified School District's (LAUSD) seniority-based staffing system, also known as "last in, first out," or LIFO, has cost the district enormous numbers of young, talented and potentially talented teachers, particularly over the last four years. This is unacceptable in the face of persistent low achievement. In LAUSD, only roughly three in five students graduate from high school in four years.[5] Among those graduates, a mere 15 percent are eligible for admission to the state's public university system, due to their poor grades and the lack of rigor in their high school coursework.[6] Beyond the economic implications of these numbers are deeply problematic questions of justice and access to excellent education. This disgraceful situation persists year after year, while nearly all of the district's teachers are rated "satisfactory" on annual evaluations. Although the district's new evaluation system will create distinctions among teachers, these ratings will not be factored into layoff decisions. California state law dictates that when layoffs are required, as they have been each of the last four years, which teachers will remain in their classrooms and which will be forced out will still be determined by one criterion, and one criterion alone: seniority.

I am one of many LAUSD teachers who was laid off and not rehired. Instead, I now work at a charter school, where I feel that I have more job security than I did when I worked for the district. Today my principal is the sole decider of staffing questions at our school. When a teacher is excellent, good, or at least making necessary improvements, that teacher is celebrated and supported. I need not fear losing my job, precisely because I have proven myself to be an effective teacher. Though some argue that arbitrary and unfair decisions by principals may cost teachers their jobs, I believe this is rare. I am more concerned that the seniority policy arbitrarily protects numerous ineffective teachers at the expense of student learning. If our system is going to be truly committed to student outcomes, the students' need for excellent teachers must trump teachers' fear of arbitrary firing. In my school, a teacher's effectiveness is more important than his or her hire date, and that ought to be the case nationwide.

Public charter schools like mine are sometimes criticized for draining students from traditional public schools, which in theory causes teacher layoffs in district schools. But I challenge this notion. In fact, the charter community was the only entity hiring when I lost my job with LAUSD. Even today, four years after I was laid off by LAUSD, I do not stand a chance of being rehired by LAUSD—even though there are many classrooms with long-term and day-to-day substitutes. This results when there are senior teachers in the district who will not take jobs at certain "undesirable" schools. The union contract dictates that schools are not allowed to hire at will when there is an opening, but instead must defer to the seniority list. When more-senior teachers refuse to take a position like the one I lost, the position goes unfilled until the bureaucratic backlog produces a credentialed teacher who is willing to take the opening. This process can sometimes take years. The bottom line: this process means that students in the highest-need schools—those children who can least afford to lose great teachers—are disadvantaged the most by LIFO.

Indeed, this was the case at my former school. My departure from Cherie and her classmates would not have been quite so disappointing if a competent teacher had taken my spot on the first day of school and continued to provide these students with quality instruction and perhaps also enrichment. Instead, when I checked back in on my classroom assignment a few weeks after my last day, I learned that a new teacher had not shown up for the start of classes. My classroom was eventually staffed by a full-time credentialed teacher, but valuable learning time was lost in the interim. The district rationalized my layoff by insisting there were many educators above me on the seniority list who deserved my job more than I did. Sadly, finding a more-senior teacher who wanted to work with Cherie, in a school in that part of town, was not an easy task, as senior teachers often do not want to work in the most difficult schools. I looked on while my former students were deprived—not just once, but multiple times—of a teacher who cared about them, as nearly half of my school's staff was laid off according to seniority that year. Without excellent teachers in front of them every single day, the likelihood that Cherie and her classmates will attain high school diplomas, much less college diplomas, diminishes day by day.

With such abysmal graduation rates, how can the district and state justify performance-blind layoff policies? Students like Cherie, who live in poverty, have the greatest need for skilled and devoted teachers because of the extra challenges they face. They should be the last to lose their teachers to budget cuts, particularly when the teachers are truly committed and produce results. A system that fails to account for teacher effectiveness when choosing who should be in the classroom is bound to produce mediocre results at best. In LAUSD's case, the results are not even mediocre; they are disturbingly inadequate. There is no other profession in this country that fails to take quality and results into account in hiring and firing decisions. It is time for the teaching profession to catch up.

RESPONSE

Celine Coggins and Lindsay Sobel

Tina C. Ahlgren's and Jeanette Marrone's experiences demonstrate the crux of the debate over seniority-based layoffs. These are powerful testimonies, but the stories are far from unusual. Ahlgren's and Marrone's perspectives—and their perseverance and leadership—reinforce what the research tells us.

Seniority is not an adequate proxy for effectiveness.

Both Ahlgren and Marrone improved significantly during their first years in the classroom. Yet even at the start of their careers, they were the kind of highly effective teachers who contribute significantly to student learning, and they had the potential to grow if given the opportunity to stay in their classrooms. Recent research demonstrates that, while teachers do increase their effectiveness during their first years of teaching, a significant number of those teachers laid off in a seniority-only system would not also be laid off in a system that accounts for performance.[7]

While the research on teacher effectiveness is persuasive and ample, its application in decision making is more complicated. If we are to prioritize teacher effectiveness measures over unambiguous measures of seniority, we need reliable systems of measuring teacher effectiveness. Historically, performance has been judged largely on principal observations, which are notoriously imperfect, given the risks of bias and lack of subject knowledge. The risks of unreliability are especially high if observations are infrequent and conducted by only one observer. The more recent wave of effectiveness measures has brought student test scores into the picture, but the research on test data demonstrates that it, too, offers a limited and imperfect window into teacher performance when used alone. For example, teachers point out that tests are often not aligned to the standards they are expected to teach and that they fail to account for the fact that many teachers work with highly mobile students who might have been in their classroom for only a few weeks before the test. The research tells us unambiguously that differences in teacher effectiveness can be evaluated most reliably through the balanced use of multiple measures, including student test score growth, classroom observations, and other metrics.[8] Following a recent wave of overhauls to teacher evaluation systems, the majority of states now require evaluations to include multiple measures of teacher effectiveness—a promising development.

Seniority-based layoffs result in more teachers losing their jobs than would be the case under a system that takes effectiveness into account.

As the evidence on the importance of teacher effectiveness in student learning was growing, state and district budgets were rapidly shrinking. The Great Recession that began in 2008 is still making its impact felt in schools throughout the country. Tax revenues in many states have not rebounded back to pre-2008 levels, forcing inevitable negative consequences for schools. Salaries and benefits, which constitute about 80 percent of an average district's budget, are almost impossible to protect from cuts.

The demographic patterns in play pose an additional challenge to district budgets. In most locations, teacher pay rises with experience through a step-and-lane system that has existed for the better part of a century. Teachers at the bottom of the salary schedule (those with the least experience) typically cost a district less than half what a teacher at the top of the salary schedule (those with the most experience) does, regardless of the quality of those teachers. Thus, with large numbers of teachers from the baby boom generation reaching the top levels of the income scale, average teacher salary is often the most challenging figure for a district official to wrestle with. And the pensions owed to retirees and near-retirees have contributed further to belt-tightening. Ahlgren tells the story of a veteran teacher who refused to teach, or even do small tasks like taking attendance—yet he was paid $30,000 more than an early career teacher. By retaining this teacher during layoffs, the district not only ensured that he would continue to impede student learning, but it paid a premium to retain him over more effective junior colleagues.

According to a *Los Angeles Times* analysis, 25 percent fewer teachers would have lost their jobs in 2009–2010 layoffs if the Los Angeles Unified School District (LAUSD) had based its cuts on a measure of teacher effectiveness rather than laying off only those at the bottom of the salary scale.[9]

Seniority-based layoffs have their greatest impact on students in low-income communities.

In 2012, approximately 20,000 California teachers received pink slips, including some 9,500 teachers in Los Angeles. It was the fourth year in a row of large-scale teacher cuts there. The state's passage of Proposition 30 brought a slowdown in teacher layoffs in 2013,[10] but those layoffs that are made continue to be based on "last in, first out" (LIFO) policies, just as thousands of teacher layoffs are in other states and districts around the country.

The schools these teachers work in serve disproportionately poor and disadvantaged populations of students. Inexperienced teachers tend to be concentrated in these schools where other teachers have fled, exacerbating the blow to the school when the least senior teachers in the district are cut from the staffing rolls—often in the middle of the year. During the 2009–2010 layoffs in LAUSD, three struggling middle schools lost more than half of their teaching staffs due to seniority-based layoffs. A class-action lawsuit was filed on behalf of students in those schools, charging that LIFO policy was a violation of equal protection under the law.[11] Jeanette Marrone's school was one of the schools deemed so vulnerable to layoffs that it was protected under a settlement in that case. (Recently, the settlement was invalidated by an appeals court, and the issue has continued to be litigated.)

The research, the fiscal crisis, and the sweeping generational change all converge in school staffing policy. Don't we as educators have a moral imperative to act on behalf of students and ensure they have the best possible teachers? Is waiting until the teacher evaluation process is perfect allowing "great" to be the enemy of "good (enough)"?

Teachers must be the leaders in solving the problems of their profession. And policy makers must take teachers' views into account as they make critical decisions for the students with whom teachers work every day. Because of the leadership of teachers like Ahlgren and Marrone, effectiveness has begun to be taken into account in reductions in force across the country. It is incumbent on all of us to ensure that this trend continues—and that districts are held accountable for establishing high-quality teacher evaluation systems that identify the teachers who are making the biggest difference for students.

5

Engaging Early Career Teachers in the Union

FRAMING THE ISSUE

Paul Toner

Change is the law of life. And those who look only to the past or present are certain to miss the future.

—John F. Kennedy

Teacher unions are under tremendous pressure to change. As President Kennedy said, if we don't embrace change, we are certain to miss the future. Changing how we operate does not mean we have to disown past successes or let go of our mission. It does mean that we cannot expect past accomplishments alone to satisfy the interests of early career teachers or the concerns expressed by the public. The demands for change are all around us.

During recent years, teachers and teacher unions have been the focus of an enormous amount of attention from various stakeholders. This has been especially true since Congress reauthorized the Elementary and Secondary Education Act (ESEA) in 2001. Since then, each state has been held accountable for making "adequate yearly progress" toward educating all students to the goal of proficiency on the state's assessment by 2014. Public schools and educators have been increasingly expected to meet the needs of every child and to overcome not only barriers encountered within the school day, but also the many obstacles to higher achievement that students face outside of the school day. This has led to increasing public debate on how best to create change to meet the urgent needs of our students, especially those in our high-poverty urban and rural districts, and on the role of teacher unions in this process.

We are also facing increased involvement of various stakeholders in local decisions. Gone are the days when most education policies were made by school committees, superintendents, and unions at the local level. The state and federal governments now set many of the significant education policies. These include designing curriculum frameworks, developing student assessments, establishing licensure tests for new teachers, requiring ongoing professional development, and most recently, mandating significant changes in the teacher and administrator evaluation systems. As the locus of power has moved outward, the numbers and types of stakeholder groups influencing education policy have mushroomed. If teacher unions do not offer our own compelling ideas, noneducators will invariably frame the debate.

There are some who believe we should simply say no to these new proposals and fight off as many changes as possible. I believe we have to be bolder and stronger in voicing our best thinking on educational issues. If we have legitimate disagreements with a proposal, we should make our reasons explicit and offer our own solutions to the problems others are seeking to solve. There is no point in demanding a voice for teachers or a seat at the table if we are not going to use the opportunity to promote our own proposals for positive change.

In addition to these policy shifts, there are demographic shifts among our own membership that have implications for the policies we design and those we support or oppose. As the baby boom generation of teachers is retiring, the percentage of early career teachers is rising. In the past decade, the demographics of the profession have shifted from a cohort dominated by teachers with significant experience to one where the majority has less than ten years of experience.[1] Many of these newer teachers have worked in other sectors of the economy before entering the field of education. Others have no personal or family history of union membership and involvement. We have to recognize that their needs, interests, and concerns are not always the same as those of their more senior colleagues.

As the demographics of the teaching force change, it is appropriate to wonder what the implications will be, particularly for the unions. Some experts have suggested that this demographic shift signals a growing generational divide within the teaching force.[2] Others have suggested that there are two generations of teachers working side by side in our schools, the "union" generation and the "professional" generation. I respectfully disagree with drawing this distinction. In order for education to become a profession within which teachers are truly given the respect, resources, meaningful decision-making roles, and autonomy we deserve, we need the collective voice and strength of our unions, and we need that voice to include early career teachers as well as veteran teachers.

How can unions better engage their earlier-career members while still meeting the needs of more veteran teachers? And what can teachers do to facilitate that change?

FROM THE CLASSROOM TO THE BIG PICTURE

Why I Changed My Mind About Teacher Unions

Karen L. McCarthy

I did not start my career concerned about the state of teacher unionism. In fact, I wanted nothing to do with it. Instead, I spent hours thinking about my lessons, worrying about the often dire social and emotional realities of many of my students, and finding people and resources to help me improve as an educator. I didn't think much about how my union helped me in my role as a teacher, and I was turned off by its image, which included stories about "rubber rooms,"[3] incompetent teachers being protected, and veterans bullying members whose opinions differed from the so-called orthodoxy. During these years of teaching a combined English and special education class in a large urban high school, I was so overwhelmed with learning to be a good teacher that I never took the time to examine my views about teacher unions. A part of me recognized that they had a place, but if I thought of them at all, it was as a necessary evil.

Eventually things changed: I married my long-time partner, bought a home, and had two children. My maternity leave and health-care benefits were critical. My salary became even more important, my planning time during school hours became more crucial to my effectiveness, and having some semblance of job security helped me to sleep at night. I began to see greater value in my union.

After I became more competent in the classroom, my interests in education grew beyond it. I began to think much more deeply about the "big picture" policy issues affecting education. I started reading more research and became informed about policy changes and innovations. As I paid more attention, I heard countless people inside and outside the field of education describing reform and those who participate in reform as polarized: the rhetoric described those on the side of "quality" education for students in opposition to those on the "other" side of the debate—the adversary of reform, the teacher unions. This didn't make sense to me. Apart from noting the obvious oversimplification, I knew that teacher unions consisted of educators whose daily mission is to provide students with a quality education. At that time, national policies such as the federal "Race to the Top" initiative and various state-level policies were challenging a lot of positions that teacher unions held. I had recently met several well-respected colleagues who were active in their union, and all of this forced me to inspect my own beliefs about teacher unions. I was also working under my third principal in less than two years, and had come to see that there was an extreme range in leadership quality across schools. It became clear to me that there needed to be an avenue for teachers to have some control over the means to improve their schools.

Around this time I also came across an interesting piece of data: I learned that the highest outcomes for students on both the National Assessment of Educational Progress (NAEP) and the SAT were correlated with the most highly unionized states. In fact, my own state of Massachusetts is both a strong union state and a high performing state in terms of student assessment results on the NAEP.[4] This information caused me to revisit my assumptions about teacher unions. I began to think about how my union helped me to be a better teacher. I recognized that it provided a vehicle for teacher voice and expertise in important decisions affecting schools, and that it ensured viable working conditions so that I could perform my job well. I came to see that unions are not in opposition to high-quality education; in fact they work to enable excellence.

GETTING INVOLVED: SEEKING LEADERSHIP

I decided to become actively involved in my union because I want to see teaching become more valued in our society. We need to attract the best and the brightest teachers into our profession and help them stay so we can truly build upon our collective talent. The union is a strong lever to achieve this goal. I realized that if I want to strengthen and improve our union, then I must become a part of it, rather than dismissing it as I had at the start of my career.

Despite this revelation, it took encouragement and role models for me to find the courage to become involved. I remember very clearly, in my third or fourth year of teaching, that a teacher I had worked alongside became a union building representative. She was dedicated and had consistently effected change with both her students and in our larger school community. More recently, another colleague whom I respected for her intelligence and innovation encouraged me to do the same—so I did. These excellent educators helped me to realize that I should practice what I preached: if I wanted my colleagues to be proud of our union, I had to be proud enough to be a visible face within it.

Then I took on a bigger challenge. I decided to run for my local union's executive board. I campaigned on a message of reclaiming our image as a union of professionals. I also spoke about the need to confront and change the stereotype that we could not be both unionized and excellent. I focused on the need to reframe the national dialogue about unions and greater issues in education, and the need for our union to become more proactive in solving the problems that hinder student achievement in our schools. I wanted to highlight the connection between positive working conditions and student success and maintaining competitive wages and benefits. I talked to people about creating more vehicles for member input into innovations and policies to improve our schools and about engaging a broader membership. I especially wanted to engage new teachers, who are fundamental to the success and future of the union, but I also wanted to connect with any disengaged members who had lost faith in our union (or had never had it). In my campaign, I shared that I had not always recognized the importance of teacher unions, and that I hoped that teachers who had been similarly disengaged might see a bit of themselves in me and my campaign and come out to vote. I must admit: at times I wavered in my commitment to running for office, and in many ways I felt very uncomfortable putting myself out there. Despite my genuine belief in the importance of teacher unions, I still worried that people would paint me with the same negative brush with which I had ignorantly painted other union-involved teachers.

Many people, including many longtime colleagues, told me that I was a long shot at best. I spoke with some veteran union members who were very experienced and knowledgeable about the political process. They told me (and I heard that they had told others) it was unlikely I could win. They didn't mean to, but they greatly discouraged my candidacy. I felt that they respected me, but they were very clear that I was not going to be able to win unless I spent at least $1500, ran a phone bank, and shook hands each morning across the district. With two young children in day care, committing a lot of money to the campaign was not an option for my family, nor was committing a great deal of time. I was also told that those established in the union would resent a newcomer making a bold move to run for such an important position. When I was tired from a long day at work and taking care of my own children, these comments—while well intended as consolation in advance should I fail—were often enough to lower my drive to campaign. I was discouraged and intimidated. I was also torn as to whom to focus on—should I focus on newer teachers who may see themselves in my change-of-heart-story, or the teachers who frequented the union meetings and could be counted on to vote?

One night I came home especially discouraged, worried that I was making a fool of myself for running. My husband turned to me and told me I was "the bravest girl [he] knew," and that at the very least I was getting a message out there. Running for office was a truly personal investment and required more courage than I had realized.

But as I began to do more outreach, I found many union members who encouraged my candidacy. Union leaders, veteran teachers, and newer teachers alike supported my platform and were positive about my campaign. Rather than dismissing my candidacy, they encouraged me. They introduced me to others at the union hall and agreed to share my flyers at their schools; some even thanked me for running and getting involved. A diverse body of teachers recognized the need to engage members who were new to union involvement. Again and again I heard "It's nice to see young people involved in the union." This was remarkable, because I am in my late thirties, certainly not a "young" teacher. In fact, I am on the more experienced end of "early career" teachers, with nine years in the classroom at the time of my campaign. The fact that I am considered "young" at the union hall underscores the point that a large portion of members, especially the early career teachers, is missing from active involvement.

I did not follow the traditional mechanisms for campaigning. The expensive "palm cards," so named because they fit in one's palm—and therefore could not hold much meaningful information—did not appeal to me as a voter, and therefore I did not invest in them as a candidate. I chose instead to print a simple flyer that gave enough information for teachers to be able to determine my values and priorities as well as my credentials, and to contact me to engage in further discussions. I made no large name signs for election day, because again, I did not see how or why simply displaying my name—without any substantive platform attached—should resonate. In lieu of a phone bank, I sent e-mails to my colleagues and contacts, hoping some would be interested in my candidacy, and engaged in one event where I was able to speak with the other candidates about my platform and to field questions.

On election day, I set my sights low. I was convinced that the best I could do was to not come in last. There are twelve positions on the executive board. I came in thirteenth—by ten votes. I could think of twenty, thirty, heck, even forty people who supported me but who had not taken the time to come out and vote. I was shocked.

In some ways, losing by only ten votes did make it more difficult to accept the loss, but on the whole the experience was overwhelmingly positive. Everything about it worked to crush any remaining stereotypes I held about my union. There was no entrenched power that would not welcome a newcomer. I did not need tremendous amounts of money (I spent $150 dollars on flyers). I realize in retrospect that I might have gained a position on the board if I had worked harder. Two other early career teachers who were new to the elections also ran for positions on the executive board. One gained a position with the fourth-highest number of votes, and the other came in fourteenth—right after me. This was a clear message that people were eager for more voices and perspectives in the union. It was also a clear signal to me, as a committed union member, that we need to do a better job of giving teachers access to their union and of increasing voter turnout.

WHERE ARE YOU IN THE UNION?

I hope that my personal story will resonate with teachers who might question their need to get involved in their union. Running was intimidating—it took a huge leap of faith, courage, and conviction, but I am glad I did it. Now it's time for other teachers to take on similar challenges. The voter turnout at my election was abysmally low—less than 15 percent of the membership. I am frustrated that folks did not make voting a priority—we must step up and take advantage of basic opportunities to be part of change. I believe that I should have worked harder, especially in regard to voter turnout, but it is very difficult to get new voters engaged if we go about business as usual; many still don't see the union as a viable avenue for effecting change that is meaningful to them. Through my campaign, I met many teachers who wanted to work to improve our profession. I saw an untapped and unrecognized force for change among us, but few who recognized our union as a significant means for collaborating and for invigorating our profession.

The labor movement is very important, but our union will be strong and visionary and create the outcomes teachers believe are important only if more of us get involved. I realize that teachers are busy. We are consumed by our work. Not everyone needs to go as far as I did; there are many ways to have a voice. Aside from running for office, all teachers can contact elected union leaders to share ideas, and they can vote in union elections so that policies reflect more union members' priorities. Union meetings are opportunities to have input when important proposals arise, or to propose new ones. At the very least, let's reexamine our beliefs and open our minds to the possibility of the union as a route to elevating our profession.

LOOKING AHEAD

Today I see teacher unions as an important collective voice for teachers in our nation. But we could do more. I am frequently disappointed and frustrated when I see unions appearing to undermine themselves. We often react instead of lead and miss opportunities to define ourselves as leaders in the effort to strengthen education. I do not want to perpetuate the belief that if we value our contract, then we do not value children. Despite much negative framing of unions in the media, I believe there is no conflict between the interests of teachers and positive outcomes for students. We need to clearly connect the work of our union with the values—such as equity, quality, and innovation—we hold most dear. We must reframe our message and our policies and take back our image as a union of professionals dedicated to advancing our field. Because of our failure to fully showcase these values and to clearly show how we build policies based on these values, a good deal of the media, policy makers and interest groups—and even some parents and teachers themselves—focus on a vocal minority in the union that is resistant to change. No teacher wants to be associated with "rubber rooms." We want teachers and our union to be associated with professionalism and excellence. To accomplish this, both the union and teachers like me, who now see value in the union, need to engage a broader membership. We need the ideas and the passion of both new teachers who are eager to embark on this career and veterans who will share their skills and experience. We need teachers of different backgrounds, perspectives, and experiences if we are to harness our collective strengths to create a sustainable teaching profession that respects teachers and serves its students.

At union meetings and during contract negotiations, I see buttons and signs saying "Unity." Every time we hold a sign or wear a pin, we are involved in a public relations opportunity that should communicate how important teachers and collective bargaining are to an effective education profession. "Unity" does not communicate our vision to the public and means little if we are not simultaneously demanding professionalism. To do this, we need to be solutions oriented. Teacher unions are just now becoming active in improving ineffective teacher evaluation systems, a problem that has plagued our profession for ages. I read critiques from my union about various measures being proposed to gauge teachers' impact. These critiques are important, but offering other solutions to gauge effectiveness would make the conversation much more productive. Union memberships contain vast amounts of expertise and experience; we can utilize this knowledge to find solutions to the problems in our schools.

The teaching profession is at a turning point. There is a lot at stake. Currently, the majority of our nation's teachers are in their first ten years of teaching. Studies show that this majority feels a similar disconnect from their union as I did.[5] This is a problem. Without these teachers' involvement, unions will surely lose strength and the potential to create change.

The call for education reform is loud. So-called reformers battle over the directions these changes should take. I largely agree that our profession needs some "modernizing," but I absolutely do not want to see this happening without teachers at the helm. What happens now will determine the course of our profession for the next decade, at least. We must bring the voice of teachers into the discourse; our union provides an established, powerful platform to do so.

Teacher unions should also continue to perform traditional union functions, such as bargaining for a contract that creates respectful working conditions, benefits, and a competitive wage for its membership. This role is inextricably linked to the success of our students. A competitive wage helps to attract strong people to and retain them in the profession. Favorable working conditions for teachers translate to smaller class sizes, healthy school buildings, and more resources for students. Yet, however central to the purpose of unions, these functions of the union are increasingly insufficient for today's teachers, who also seek a vehicle to improve the profession and move it forward. If there is one thing I have come to realize in my ten years of teaching, it is that the expertise and brainpower in our schools is woefully underutilized to solve the problems within them, and that there are droves of teachers who would welcome an opportunity to give input into reforms and policies. If our unions do not have these avenues, we must demand they create them.

I believe that teacher unions are open to meaningful reform that is respectful of both teachers and the students they serve. I leave this experience hopeful. I am more convinced than ever that the union is good not only for teachers, but also for students. I feel inspired to fight the stereotypes that I used to hold. Let us confront and change the view that teachers cannot embrace both their unions and excellence.

Addendum: Since this writing, the author went on to colead an effort to change the voting procedures in the Boston Teachers Union, expanding voting access to a wider range of union members through the use of mail-in ballots. A measure was approved to allow absentee ballots in September 2012.

CAUGHT IN THE MIDDLE VERSUS FINDING THE MIDDLE GROUND

What's Best for the Children of Chicago?

Gina Caneva

Early on in my career, I was aware of the union only because it took dues out of my paycheck. The union seemed to be an invisible entity then, one that seemed more important to protecting my older colleagues. I often asked my colleagues if I should stay in the union, and they always countered that I would need my union in times of crisis.

I taught for the next seven years without strong ties to my union or to my district. My district's focus on high-stakes testing disturbed me, and my union's insistence on an unwavering tenure system and pay scale that protected and rewarded all teachers, even the mediocre and ineffective ones, disheartened me. I was a compliant member of both my union and my district, but I didn't believe that either knew what was best for the children of Chicago. I kept on teaching my students in Englewood with the best strategies I knew, even though I would be treated the same as the teacher next door, who constantly talked on her cell phone. I continued onward until, sure enough, a time of crisis.

Last spring, I attended several union meetings where my union representative spoke about Mayor Rahm Emanuel's plan to increase the hours of the school day without giving teachers a wage increase. I am a proponent of the longer school day, because I know how far behind many Chicago students are compared to their suburban peers. Time and time again, research has shown that effective use of instructional time has a significant impact on student learning.[6] But I was opposed to the district's proposed wage freeze and proposed increase in teacher contributions to our benefits due to the high cost of living in Chicago, where Chicago Public Schools (CPS) employees are required to live. Chicago Teachers Union (CTU) leaders told us the union would be gearing up for a strike. September inched closer, and the district's and mayor's rhetoric began to make me feel that my role as a teacher was being devalued, while my union's rhetoric became one of social justice, of fighting for teachers' rights to better conditions in our schools. Both motivated me to vote for the strike.

With the strike, I felt that my union echoed my views on the importance of protecting the middle class and the rights of workers. Ever since I became a teacher and a union member, wages, pensions, affordable health care, and job protection seem to have gone by the wayside in the private sector. In recent years, the public sector has seen these rights diminish as well, and very few of us are able to do anything about it. A close relative did not have a voice when a CEO took most of her pension away at a major corporation. Another relative could do little as his public sector employer asked him to take furlough days. My friends remain powerless as their private employers hike up their costs for health insurance. Too many of us in this country remain voiceless because the fight is too big to take on alone. The CTU, built on the principles of workers' rights and equal pay for minorities and women, fought for me.

The strike made me truly feel like a union member, and I was proud to stand side by side with my colleagues in the fight for better education for my students. Many of us became caught up in the camaraderie, the rhetoric, and yes, the spectacle of it all. But in spite of my belief in the strike and my conviction that the union has played and continues to play an important historical role in upholding the middle class in America, I continue to find myself in conflict with my union too. In order to fix Chicago's schools, our union must lead efforts both to improve working conditions *and* to look critically at teacher performance alongside seniority in hiring practices and compensation.

The CPS are not serving their students as well as they need to. Only 8 percent of African American students who attend CPS, for example, graduate from college within six years.[7] We have to do better than this, and my union's positions on tenure, compensation, and career ladders restrain the education system in Chicago from constantly improving the quality of education for its students.

I saw this problem early on. I began my career at a neighborhood high school ranked sixty-eighth out of seventy on the far South Side of Chicago. I was as green as they come, but I managed to have steady classroom management and was content savvy enough to attempt to help my students become better readers and writers. I made somewhere close to $40,000 my first year, a pretty competitive number for a first-year teacher even for a suburban district—a salary my union had fought for.

During first period, I had a very small class, and it was located next door to a teacher who had twenty or more years on the job. She often showed up twenty to twenty-five minutes late, and I would take her students into my classroom so they wouldn't be without a teacher in the meantime. She would show up, thank me, take the students back to her classroom and teach them for the remaining fifteen minutes. Due to the protections and salary schedules that my union had also fought for, that teacher made at least $30,000 more than I did.

In this instance and many others that I've experienced, the union has put its workers' rights over students' rights. Every time my union defends an ineffective teacher, argues that more experience automatically means more effectiveness, or claims that creating a career ladder for teachers will create a rift between union members, I inch a step away from aligning with the union.

The CTU and CPS need to compromise on areas of tenure, pay scales, and career ladders, because this is the right thing to do for both teachers and students. Tenure has the potential to become an incentive system for improving one's teaching practice. It could even be set up as a five-tier system, where a protection or incentive is added per tier, instead of all-inclusive protections being granted after four years of teaching. And what about the rest of one's career? What's the motivation to keep improving? Besides offering incentives for improvement, we also need to reduce the time we allow ineffective teachers to remain in the classroom from ninety days to thirty days. Ninety days is just too much lost instructional time if an underperforming teacher is not showing signs of improvement.

In the area of compensation, the CTU and CPS should give teachers options. Some teachers may want to opt into a performance pay structure, while others may prefer the traditional step-and-lane system. Under the new contract, only the step-and-lane-system is enabled. There is no reason why teachers can't have a choice in the matter. Lastly, in the area of career ladders, the CTU and CPS need to compromise and make a solid effort to retain effective teachers by creating pathways to leadership. Currently, a high school department chair is rewarded with more work, no pay increase, and no guaranteed classes off to manage his or her added responsibilities. Many teachers find that they've become leaders in title only, and subsequently leave their leadership post after a short while, as there is no incentive to stay. The result is a revolving door of teacher leadership, draining stability from the schools that need it most.

More solutions-oriented, nuanced thinking on these issues would allow me to embrace both my union and my district more wholeheartedly. However, many months after the strike, ambivalence continues to nag me as I teach my students. I wear red on Fridays in support of my union, but my real hope is that the union and the district will one day meet in the middle to be more effective for our students.

RESPONSE

Paul Toner

As we have read in Karen L. McCarthy's and Gina Caneva's pieces, the issues we are trying to solve are very complex. While veteran and newer teachers may share many of the same goals and interests, there may also be differences. We must be conscious of these differences, where they exist, and encourage newer members to seek leadership positions in the ranks of our unions at the local, state, and national levels. If we do not, they may well question whether they want to continue to be dues-paying members and, rather than become active in their union, may find other methods to express their priorities and values in our schools.

Recent research highlights the areas of similarity and difference. More time for teacher collaboration and planning and the importance of small class sizes are areas where teachers tend to agree, regardless of number of years in the classroom. On the other hand, early-career teachers tend to be more in favor of linking compensation to performance, for example, than are their more experienced colleagues.[8] The Massachusetts Teachers Association's (MTA) internal membership polling similarly demonstrates that early-career teachers are almost twice as likely to strongly or somewhat favor the use of evaluation results in determining teacher pay and bonuses on top of teachers' base salaries.[9] These differences are precisely the sort that union leaders must pay attention to. Indeed, we must bring early career teachers to the table so we understand them better and can design and negotiate policies that meet their needs.

As McCarthy's and Caneva's pieces illuminate, generational gaps are evident not only with regard to specific policies, but also in attitudes toward the union more broadly. Two years ago, I joined a panel discussion with Richard Stutman, president of the Boston Teachers Union (BTU). We spoke with a group of early career teachers, primarily from Boston, about what they see as their role in the union. Using live polling technology, the teachers weighed in on questions about the union and their involvement with it. The data made it clear that there is a gap between these early career teachers' perceptions of the purpose and function of the union and the work and policies that their unions currently pursue. For example, 59 percent appreciated that their union protects their rights, but only 13 percent agreed that their union clearly aligns with and represents their points of view.[10] While this data could undoubtedly vary with different pools of teachers, in this case it was very clear from the conversations that followed that these early career teachers wanted their union to put forward a professional image and a proactive agenda with the primary objective of supporting their efforts to improve student achievement.

These teachers, as well as teachers in other cities across the country, argue for reform within the union and a realignment of priorities, and they want to advocate for this work as union leaders. They want professional compensation and good benefits, but they question longstanding education policies and practices. I personally support the involvement of early career teachers in union leadership and have made a concerted effort to recruit and appoint new members into positions of leadership at the local, state, and national levels. The MTA has an established New Members and Emerging Leaders Program at our Summer Leadership Conference every year. Many new leaders, myself included, have come out of these programs and taken on leadership roles in their local, state, and national unions.

Any time I have had the opportunity to speak with educators, especially newer members, I have emphasized the importance of their becoming active in their union. If they believe that their union is not speaking for them, they should get involved and run for a leadership position, which is exactly what I did in my local association. This is also what McCarthy describes. In the spring of 2011, McCarthy and three other Boston Public Schools teachers and Teach Plus Teaching Policy Fellows decided that, in order to make the changes they sought in the BTU, they should assume leadership roles themselves. They decided to run for the executive board of the BTU. The teachers differed in their positions and purposes, but they were united in one belief: if you want to see the change, you have to "be the change." Similarly, in an unrelated undertaking in Los Angeles, early career teachers organized themselves into a group called NewTLA to campaign for union leadership positions as candidates interested in promoting reform from within the union. The coalition gained eighty-three seats in the union's house of representatives. As union leaders, we need to encourage and cultivate these new and enthusiastic members.

As teacher unions, we need to be bolder in promoting our own ideas for improving schools and more aggressive in publicizing these positions. This is why, in the past few years, the MTA has increasingly stepped out publicly in support of efforts to improve labor-management relationships and to implement the Expanded Learning Time Initiative and initiatives such as the federal "Race to the Top" grant program, and has developed and promoted our own vision of a new framework of educator evaluation.[10] In addition, the National Education Association and the American Federation of Teachers have increasingly come forward with proposals on the issues of evaluation, compensation, and improving underperforming schools. In order to be successful, we have to work harder at being open to new ideas and to attracting and engaging our own members in these conversations, especially our newer members. I hope that in some small way this chapter will help open up the conversation between the generations of teachers—early career teachers and their veteran colleagues—and broaden the discussion within and outside the profession.

As MTA president, I believe it is important for my union—and for unions in other states—to remain a leading voice on labor issues and to be a strong advocate for public education employees while simultaneously promoting policies that strengthen and improve the profession. Teacher unions must position themselves to lead the conversation for positive change in order to improve our schools and support our students. Where there are challenges to be addressed, such as the significant achievement gaps among our students, we must not shy away from policies that could significantly benefit students. That means speaking out about poverty, revenues, and a host of other social issues. It also means working hard to ensure that we are part of the solution at every step along the way. We must present our models of educator-led change. Teachers and their unions should be the architects of reform, not the objects of it. It is our challenge—and an opportunity for our members—to recruit, train, and support a new cadre of local activists from among the early career teachers, those who might bring a broader array of interests to bear and who would like to tackle some of the nontraditional issues.

Not long ago, the American public watched events unfold in several states—including Wisconsin, Indiana, and Ohio—where legislatures and governors issued proposals to do away with collective bargaining, tenure, and other job protections. As this occurred, it became apparent that not only were teacher unions facing challenges from their own members on policies for which they had long fought, but also that the public at large was divided on the future of unions in the public sector. If the unions do not tackle some of these issues (e.g., revamping teacher evaluation, defining excellence, and reimagining compensation), there will continue to be an appetite for dismantling the protections that unions and teachers have fought to obtain. Further, the unions will risk losing the commitment and interest of their early career teachers—those who increasingly make up the new majority of the teaching force and union membership.

Some of these early career teachers are actually stepping up to try to become leaders in the union and to forge a path that aligns policies to promote student learning and teaching as a profession. If early career teachers want to see the union align its policies with their own vision for the profession, then they must be leaders in the union. Like thoughtful union leaders across the country, these teachers view the union as a means by which they can increase the status of their profession and use collective action to bring about lasting change—for the good of teachers and the good of their students.

6

Building School Leadership That Facilitates Great Teaching

FRAMING THE ISSUE

Benjamin Fenton and Terrence Kneisel

We can all conjure up an image of a school principal. For some, the principal is the disciplinarian, the person whose office you dread being sent to, much like the principal in *The Breakfast Club*. For others, the principal is the motivational but polarizing speaker who pushes students to success—the *Lean on Me* model. And for many, the principal represents the building manager, a friendly and supportive presence in the hallways, at bus drop-offs, and in attendance at athletic events.

Although those archetypes are firmly embedded in our minds from years of personal experience and cultural acclimation, our research demonstrates that highly effective principals who are leading improvement in high-need schools are very different from those models. These principals are more likely to be found leading teacher teams through reviews of student work and instructional plans, poring over data on student progress with their leadership team, or leading student assemblies that celebrate students who exemplify the school's values.

A decade of research supports the premise of the principal's critical role in shaping the quality of instruction and learning in a school.[1] In fact, the research shows that a principal accounts for 25 percent of a school's total impact on student achievement,[2] and that the difference in student achievement under a principal with average effectiveness and one with high effectiveness can be as much as twenty percentage points.[3] The research also highlights that these estimates of impact are likely even larger for the highest-need schools.

We also know that principals drive success almost exclusively by supporting ever-increasing teacher effectiveness. The greatest principals have a laserlike focus on recruiting, hiring, developing, and retaining great teachers in their schools. In order to unleash the full power and potential of strong teachers, we must have principals doing all of these things well. We have all experienced firsthand the influence a remarkable teacher can have. It is the principal's primary job to ensure that there is a remarkable teacher in every classroom in a school, that those teachers receive the professional development they need to grow, and that the strongest teachers stay in the classroom leading and enlightening students.

The teacher retention component is incredibly important. Recent research has highlighted the principal's impact on the retention of effective teachers. A survey of more than 40,000 teachers nationwide found that 96 percent of teachers rated supportive leadership as either absolutely essential or very important to retaining good teachers—more than any other factor.[4] In addition, TNTP's report *The Irreplaceables: Understanding the Real Retention Crisis in America's Urban Schools* found that principals make too little effort to retain their highest performing educators, and that principals' actions have a significant impact on a teacher's decision to remain in the classroom and in their school 70 percent of the time.[5]

Given the critical role principals play in increasing teacher effectiveness and retaining teachers who are leading students to academic success, we recommend that the measure of a principal's quality should focus not only on the student outcomes they achieve, but also on their ability to increase the effectiveness of teachers and retain effective teachers over time.

What actions can principals take to achieve this? What qualities do teachers identify as critical for their development and retention? And what are the implications of this for principal development and evaluation?

I WASN'T READY TO STOP IMPROVING

Why Irreplaceable Teachers Need Irreplaceable Leaders

Allison Frieze

When I was rated "highly effective" by IMPACT, the District of Columbia Public Schools' (DCPS) evaluation system, I received a one-time salary bonus of $15,000. While the extra money was welcome, there were costs to this distinction. My rating acted as a permission slip for my school to cut off the coaching support that had helped me improve my teaching in the first place. For the evaluations that followed, I was videotaped rather than observed in person, and I received my scores in writing rather than during a feedback-driven conference. As far as the leadership of my school was concerned, I was a great teacher, and I could carry on with business as usual.

But I wasn't ready to stop improving—so I found a school where the leaders would still push me to do that.

I started my career teaching special education in a "low performing" district public school in Anacostia, the neighborhood with the highest unemployment and violent crimes rates in Washington, DC. Last June, I left to take a job at E. L. Haynes Public Charter School to teach the same grades and students with very similar needs. I'm a teacher the district lost.

I'm not alone in this. According to TNTP, nearly two-thirds of highly effective teachers who leave their teaching positions do so to teach in nearby schools in similar or identical roles.[6] In other words, most of us aren't leaving for other careers, or even for "easier" teaching jobs. Our school leaders just aren't giving us reasons to stay.

The impact of these moves on students can't be overstated. In their 2012 report *The Irreplaceables: Understanding the Real Retention Crisis in America's Urban Schools*, TNTP found that when a high performing teacher leaves a low performing school, only one in eleven potential replacements will be of similar quality, almost guaranteeing that when a great teacher leaves, his or her replacement will be less effective. And great teachers matter: a highly effective teacher imparts five to six months' more learning per year than an average teacher.

Across the board, teacher turnover has a negative impact on school cultures and communities. Research shows that high rates of teacher turnover negatively affect school morale and diminish student achievement, even for students whose teachers stay put.[7] School communities in constant flux aren't good for kids, and the worst effects are seen in schools that already have the lowest achievement rates.

So many high performing teachers leaving urban schools should be a red flag to school districts, signaling leadership failure. Why aren't more teachers staying put? To retain what TNTP refers to as our "irreplaceable" teachers—teachers performing in the top 10 percent of the profession, as measured by student growth data—we need irreplaceable leadership, too.

Irreplaceable school leaders know how to keep their best teachers motivated and hungry for growth. In a case study of teacher retention in DCPS, TNTP notes that many teachers identified as high performers did not experience two particular retention strategies: critical feedback and identification of areas for development.

At once a joy and a challenge for teachers is the constant effort to improve. For educators, hours of hard work do not always produce the desired results with our students. We need administrators and trained observers who will be honest about what they see and take the time to analyze and tease apart the nuances of daily practice that impact student performance. All teachers should also be given the opportunity to develop skills in self-identified or observer-identified areas for improvement.

High performing teachers are no different. We want opportunities to lead and help other teachers, but we also want support for and frequent feedback on our own performance. Instead, we are often left alone in our classrooms and denied any share of limited coaching supports and resources. This was exactly the issue I faced after my second year in the classroom. Even though I had been rated highly effective by IMPACT, I still felt that I had plenty to learn—and I was no longer receiving opportunities or support to do so. As a novice teacher, I still encountered daily behavioral challenges and felt the stress of planning units and differentiated lessons across multiple subjects. I still questioned whether my instructional choices were the best decisions for my students. I worried that my struggles reflected deeper issues in my teaching, and I became increasingly frustrated as I expressed this concern and was told over and over again that I was a great teacher. When principals assume that high-fliers cannot or do not need to improve, they not only do us (and our students) a disservice, they also run the risk of losing us. It is a fatal leadership decision. "Irreplaceables" demand excellence: we won't settle for any form of mediocrity from our students or, especially, from ourselves.

My current school guides all teachers in developing yearly "SMART goals" for our own professional development. Using our previous evaluations, we identify areas for growth and develop specific goals aligned to our school's Teacher Competency Rubric. Through observations and weekly conferences, supervisors monitor progress toward these goals and share feedback. This ensures not only that we feel in control of our development, but also that we receive differentiated development support targeted to our needs.

Teachers often cite poor school culture as a key reason for leaving. But what makes a great school culture? A commitment to continuous learning and development is one piece. And great leaders build trust between teachers and administrators by creating a dialogue around school change that encourages equity of voice and a sense of ownership and empowerment for everyone on staff. This may be accomplished through teacher-led school committees on family engagement, staff development, and social-emotional learning. To stay on top of staff culture, principals and instructional leaders should make weekly or biweekly efforts to meet with all teachers. Working conditions surveys such as the Teaching and Learning Conditions Survey by the New Teacher Center can also be used to monitor instructional culture at school and district levels.[8] In order to raise the bar for the teaching profession, and to keep our most high performing, ambitious teachers in the classroom, all teachers' effectiveness must be developed, and teachers' voices must be heard and valued on matters affecting individual school cultures and work environments.

TNTP recommends that school leaders set out to retain 90 percent or more of their high performing teachers each year.[9] Our leaders must be held accountable in their own performance ratings for keeping great teachers. Retention efforts should be incentivized for principals, with those who meet retention goals perhaps receiving financial bonuses or priority in hiring teachers who have been reassigned from other schools.

To meet the goal of retaining their best teachers year after year, superb school leaders have to have grit—the commitment and determination to achieve a goal, no matter what it takes. The principal with grit sets end-of-the-year retention goals for high performing teachers. This principal does not see or acknowledge inaction or failure or silence as options. This principal pushes every teacher to his or her full potential. Finally, this principal asks, "What is it going to take to keep you here?"

PUTTING MY BELIEFS INTO PRACTICE

Principal Leadership Makes the Difference

Audrey Herzig Jackson

I wanted to teach at the Manning Elementary School after one phone call. The Manning's incoming principal, Ethan d'Ablemont Burnes, reached out to me, explained his vision for a fully inclusive school, and asked if I would be part of putting that set of beliefs into practice. He was open and honest about the challenges of educating kids who are often underserved, and yet was most hopeful about the positive outcomes a team of educators could create. The school where I was teaching at the time was in a state of uncertainty due to a change in leadership, and I welcomed the opportunity to be part of an innovative model of schooling for a broad range of children within Boston Public Schools.

Four years into teaching at the Manning, I am very glad that I made the jump into a new, uncharted approach to inclusive teaching. The Manning technically has two classes per grade: one is a traditional classroom, and the second consists of a smaller group of children who are labeled "emotionally impaired" (EI). Phrases like "having experienced trauma, abuse, and neglect" or "behaviorally and emotionally challenged" are often used to describe these students. Unlike other Boston Public Schools with an EI strand (or indeed, most such schools nationally), our school does not separate EI students from their peers, unless there is a temporary need to do so for safety. The "regular" education teachers and "EI" teachers combine classes all day, every day—our students are not separated for instruction based on behavior labels—and work together to meet the needs of all students.

To ensure equal education access, we believe and reinforce the premise that academic limitations are not inherently part of EI students' diagnoses, and we provide substantially separate time only when it is truly needed (and then for the shortest time possible). A child who gets upset about a wrong answer and lies face down on the floor, refusing to move or speak, or another who flips tables and runs off-campus in response to losing five minutes of recess, isn't always served well in a traditional classroom. At our school, these behaviors aren't necessarily any easier to deal with, but we have a sense of purpose in persevering because we have a comprehensive plan in place to help students with these kinds of challenges make progress over time.

Of course, the work is never easy. So what has kept me from leaving this challenging school setting? My principal.

In part, our full inclusion model works because our principal trusts his teachers and collaborates with us. Over the last four years, the Manning has evolved from having pockets of inclusive practices to using full inclusion schoolwide. This shift was accomplished through reflective planning that included teachers' input and collaboration throughout, rather than with a set of sweeping changes mandated from above all at once. d'Ablemont Burnes has allowed each teacher team to develop the best model to meet the needs of its particular students, as long as the strategy aligns with the school's core beliefs about inclusion. Just as we meet our students where they are, d'Ablemont Burnes works with each teacher team to improve our inclusive planning and practices based on where we are.

When it comes to the school's budget, staffing, resource allocations, curriculum implementation, and more, our principal reaches out to teachers for solutions. He gives us flexibility to think outside the box to get the results that we all want for our students. For example, when Fernando (not his real name) was repeatedly exhibiting negative behaviors at recess and normal consequences weren't prompting change, the principal allowed us to have Fernando and a friend switch their recess and lunch schedule so that they were taking recess separate from the other students. After just two weeks, Fernando was able to develop a feeling of success at recess and was then able to rejoin his classmates. That kind of willingness to find—and test—productive solutions to problems helps us stay focused on the greater goal of helping all of our students regulate their behavior so as to be able to engage positively in all aspects of school life. My principal's proactive approach to problem solving gives me faith that when I come to a challenge that I can't solve on my own, my concerns won't be dismissed without consideration.

Teachers are not the only stakeholders whose voices are valued at the Manning: family perspectives are validated as well. Manning parents have long wanted the school expanded to eighth grade so that their children could be served by our full-inclusion setting all the way through middle school. To move this goal forward, d'Ablemont Burnes reached out to staff to generate buy-in and build a collective, community-driven vision for the school's future. He has remained undeterred in pursuing this goal, in spite of encountering numerous roadblocks, precisely because the long-term goal comes from within the school community and has been developed by considering what is best for our students.

With strong leadership, our school has proven that it's possible to fully include EI students in a regular classroom setting, given strategic supports. Is this incredibly difficult at times? Yes. Do big risks often make room for big rewards? Yes. And when it comes to children, it's important to generate hope for positive change. If education is to serve as a tool for social justice, it is vital to ensure that children who face incredibly challenging childhood circumstances have access to a rewarding and rich education.

d'Ablemont Burnes shares my conviction that education should serve as a means to achieving social justice. Having this shared purpose helps me overcome daily challenges because we have both a set of beliefs behind our work and an active plan to keep reflecting, refining, and making progress. While our work is not perfect, sharing a larger belief about the role of our school in our children's lives means that we cannot let the little things get in the way of the greater goal. At the core of the "American dream" is the belief that, with hard work, any child can grow up to be successful and happy. If this is to be true, our education system has to embody this and put it into action. Children who have mental illness or who have experienced trauma cannot be kept separated with the hope that they will magically integrate into society successfully as they age. Our school system should prepare children to be empathetic, positive contributors to society. Inclusion is built upon the belief that all children have something to contribute and all children benefit from seeing that they and their peers can create a dynamic and positive community—together. Our principal has applied the same approach to the adults in our school community that we use to support children to grow from where they are and to develop the teamwork and reflective skills they need in order to progress. With this leadership approach, our school has thrived.

HONORING MY MOTHER

The Evolution of an Unlikely Educator

Jeremy Robinson

When I was three years old, my mother piled her children into the family station wagon, drove to a pay phone at a nearby grocery store, and dialed 9-1-1. "What should a woman do who has five kids and no place to live?"

she asked. Shortly thereafter, following the advice of the emergency operator who answered my mother's call, we moved into the Salvation Army Women's Shelter in downtown Indianapolis.

Within three months, my mother had managed to secure a second-grade teaching job and convince a landlord to rent her a small house. She would be resuming her career in the classroom, and we would be resuming our lives in a place we could call home.

As my childhood unfolded and the full measure of my mother's difficult decision to raise us on her own became apparent to me, I discovered that I wanted to model myself after her in every way possible—except one. I wanted nothing to do with her chosen profession. From a very early age, I knew in my bones that I did not want to grow up to become a teacher.

But here I am. It took two organizations and, in particular, one principal's incredible leadership to finally convince me of what my mother knew all along: teaching is the most important work a person can do.

As a child, my rationale for avoiding the teaching profession seemed entirely straightforward. My mother had sacrificed immensely to offer me a better life. As a result, I had an obligation to honor her by doing better than she had done. "Doing better" meant doing something other than becoming a teacher—because becoming a teacher, in my mind, just did not seem all that impressive.

Then, as a college senior, I was handed a copy of *One Day, All Children*, Wendy Kopp's story of founding Teach For America and leading the organization through its first decade. As I delved into the book, my understanding of my mother and her life's work as a teacher went through a profound transformation. Kopp's description of the disturbing inequalities in schools across the United States stirred in me a desire to create change. Her claim that children deserve teachers who are among the best and brightest our nation can produce struck me as irrefutable. But perhaps most significant of all, Kopp's belief in the supreme importance of teachers and of the need to elevate the profession in the eyes of society debunked my childhood conviction that teaching was not and never would be for me.

As I stepped into the role of a ninth-grade English teacher at Harper High School on the South Side of Chicago, Teach for America echoed to me time and again the refrain that my job was worthy of deep respect. And it matched those affirmations with high expectations for results. Teach for America demanded continuous improvement by scrutinizing my curriculum planning and classroom management—by consistently nudging me to accept nothing short of my best effort in the pursuit of giving my students the education they deserved. Harper, on the other hand, struggled to do the same. No doubt the school's leadership yearned to create a community where teachers felt honored, where they felt challenged to grow and develop their craft. Sadly, however, it never materialized. In the end, I had to look outside the school for leadership and direction.

During my second year in the classroom, my life changed unexpectedly. I was awarded a Rhodes Scholarship to study for two years at the University of Oxford. On my last day of the school year, I thought I would never teach again.

A year and a half later, in the final stages of completing my degree, I received an e-mail from the principal of Rauner College Prep, a campus of the Noble Network of Charter Schools in Chicago. He had asked the members of his staff to write a list of the best teachers they knew, and I was on someone's list. His aim was to entice each of us to apply for a job. As a Rhodes Scholar, I now had a host of opportunities available to me. Unlike at the end of college or during my years as a ninth-grade English teacher, I was in high demand. But to the surprise of many around me, I replied that I would be open to learning why teaching at his school would be a compelling pursuit. Instead of attempting to persuade me, he invited me to see for myself.

I traveled the roughly 4,000 miles from England back to the city where my teaching career had started, assuming all the while that I knew exactly what I would encounter. I thought my two years of teaching on Chicago's South Side had exposed me to the harsh reality of what was possible—and not possible—in public education. I thought that teaching in low-income communities with the aim of making educational experiences for all children more fair and equal was heroic but ultimately unsustainable. What I witnessed at this principal's school, however, completely surprised me.

As I walked through its halls and observed in its classrooms, I realized that Rauner was doing something special. It was providing all of its students with the real possibility of getting into and graduating from college. It was equipping them with the skills and knowledge needed to pursue a life of choice rather than one preordained by poverty. It was instilling in them strong character and self-discipline. And it was doing this, in large part, because of a great school leader who valued great teaching.

Now in my fifth year as a teacher in the Noble Network, I better understand the ingredients that have contributed to its success—and that have kept me in the classroom. Chief among them is what I had realized on my first visit to Rauner: the great care with which Noble selects the principals who run its schools and, likewise, the great care with which Noble principals carry out their jobs. This is best embodied by Eric Thomas, the principal who encouraged me to give teaching another chance, and quite possibly the best leader for whom I have ever worked.

Enter the principal's office at Rauner and you will see a blue sign emblazoned on the wall with a quote from Tim Quinn of the Broad Superintendents Academy. It reads: "I ask that you come to these jobs as servants. Your singular goal is to clear away everything else so that magic can happen between teachers and students." Thomas's decision to display this quote in the precise location where his leadership team makes the majority of its decisions is meant to assert the administrative ethos of the building: the work that teachers do is primary, and all else is secondary.

Flowing naturally from this institutional belief is Thomas's obsession with ensuring that only the best educators earn a spot at the helm of one of his classrooms. He once revealed that when the school has open positions, he spends roughly 75 percent of his time researching, recruiting, and selecting "The Dream Team," as he affectionately calls his staff. Moreover, he frequently says, "It's easier to get into Harvard than it is to get a job here," a message that reinforces the shared conviction among Rauner teachers that they belong to a distinguished school and, more important, an honorable profession.

Teachers who survive the rigorous selection process quickly discover they are part of a mission-driven organization that insists unapologetically on results. Simply put, the goal is to produce college graduates who will go on to lead exemplary lives. Yet, these teachers also discover that within this demanding environment they are endowed with a refreshing degree of autonomy. Thomas acknowledges that teachers with a proven track record of effectiveness deserve the decision-making power to determine how they structure their curricula, plan their daily lessons, and ultimately ensure that all students learn. He is fond of saying, "At Rauner, we focus on results." Fortunately, teachers find they have the freedom to figure out the methods they will use to achieve those results. They feel trusted with tough decisions rather than micromanaged or second-guessed. In a school with such a highly professional culture, teachers' creativity and ingenuity are unleashed.

Teachers also find they have access to pathways that nurture and support their ongoing pedagogical growth as well as their leadership development.

Thomas invites the most effective teachers to join the school's Instructional Leadership Team and taps them to run content-area departments, grade-level teams, or advisory teams. Thomas ensures that a flat career trajectory for teachers is simply not an option—continuous professional maturation is the expectation and the norm.

In addition, teachers realize, perhaps for the first time in their careers, that they can teach in a school where working hard, achieving results, and having fun are not mutually exclusive. Thomas spurs his staff to operate with the "J-Factor"—with joy. Students, after all, deserve teachers who will awaken their deepest interests and ignite their fieriest passions. A staff that does not feel joyful will not create joyful students. So Thomas creates contexts in which teachers can get to know one another personally as well as professionally by, for example, opening up his home for occasional social gatherings or encouraging staff to participate in local athletic events together. Such seemingly small gestures tighten the bonds within the Rauner community—they weave joy into the lives of teachers so that teachers can weave joy into the lives of their students.

Perhaps most important of all, teachers discover that their principal models through his own actions the very behaviors he expects from students and staff alike. Teachers respect and trust Thomas, and as a result, work relentlessly to fulfill the vision he has set for the school. Teachers enter the building each day knowing they are lining up behind a leader who is working with the same level of effort and integrity as they are—something that gives teachers the fuel they need to sustain them on the difficult path of providing a consistently excellent educational experience for their students.

At the core of its success, the Noble Network is filled with principals like Thomas who leave nothing to chance. They are fiercely intentional about creating schools that operate with the belief that truly transformational change will happen only when great teachers are given the right conditions in which to do their jobs—even if some of those teachers never thought they would grow up to become one.

RESPONSE

Benjamin Fenton and Terrence Kneisel

Allison Frieze, Audrey Herzig Jackson, and Jeremy Robinson all highlight how important it is for leaders to focus on teacher effectiveness and retention. If we're going to attract, develop, and, especially, retain the high-quality teachers we need at scale, leaders will have to demonstrate many of the practices that were so perfectly illustrated in the reflections of these three educators.

The teachers' reflections here mirror what the broader research tells us. At New Leaders, our primary work is in recruiting and training talented individuals who will become transformational school leaders and, in turn, studying what the most effective of those leaders are doing to achieve dramatic gains for students. The recent report published by New Leaders, *Playmakers: How Great Principals Build and Lead Great Teams of Teachers*, points to three key areas of school leaders' work: developing teachers, managing talent, and creating a great place to work.[10] From these categories, we identified a number of specific actions principals take to increase teacher effectiveness (see figure 6.1).

We found that principals who led the highest gaining schools focused on at least one action in each of the major categories. Most highly effective principals viewed developing their teachers as one of their greatest priorities. They worked explicitly to improve instruction by conducting observations, providing feedback, leading professional development, focusing on data-driven instruction, and insisting on high expectations for all students. As principals are also responsible for managing the human capital at their school, the most successful principals we studied focused on hiring effective teachers, matching staff strengths with school needs, and holding teachers accountable. Finally, successful principals fostered establishment of a community among colleagues that reinforced the value of each teacher, and they eventually delegated leadership and responsibility so that teachers were given greater ownership of school decisions.

The three teachers' experiences illustrate several of the particular leadership actions in practice. They are a profound testament to the power of a principal in supporting teacher effectiveness and delivering high-quality instruction, and they provide us clear connections between the experiences of teachers in many different schools and the critical actions we know principals need to be taking.

FIGURE 6.1
Actions principals take to increase teacher effectiveness

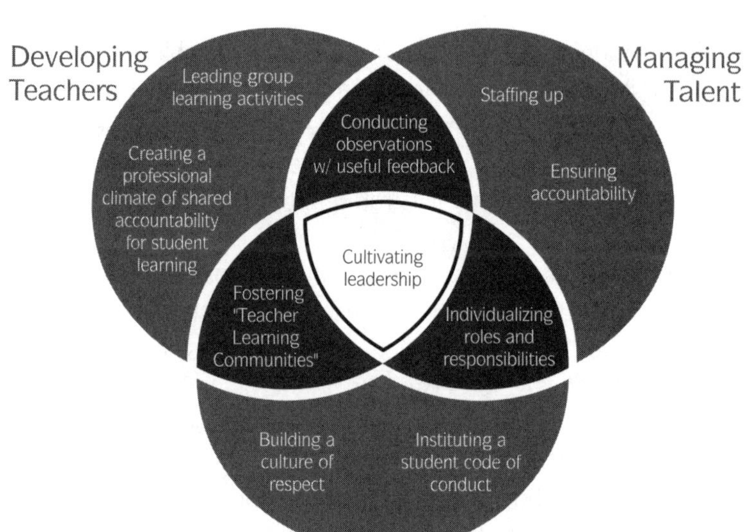

From Allison Frieze at E. L. Haynes Public Charter School, we heard about a school leadership team that ensures that all teachers, regardless of tenure or previous evaluations, receive regular feedback, support, and a push to continue growing and developing. This is a prime example of "conducting observations with useful feedback." Like Frieze's principal, the most highly effective principals in our research provide teachers with feedback throughout the school year, not just during performance evaluations. By doing this, principals are able to have a fundamental understanding of what is happening in every classroom throughout the school. Most of these principals take the time to establish norms and create a culture of understanding on how observations will be conducted, and to train their leadership teams to conduct them as well.

More important than their merely conducting observations, though, is effective principals' providing teachers with precise, actionable feedback on a regular basis. The observation itself may take only a few minutes, but the strongest principals are quick to provide direct feedback on a particular practice or set of practices, and will check on the implementation of that feedback in their next observation. We've heard firsthand from Frieze how integral the cycle of observation and feedback was to her own growth as an already highly rated educator interested in continuously improving her craft.

At the Manning Elementary School, we saw how important it is to create a "climate of shared accountability" and to ensure high expectations for all students, regardless of their past performance or challenges, which in turn allows for greater collaboration and more effective problem solving. Our research shows that by doing this, exceptional principals rally their teams of teachers and other staff members around a vision of success for all students, inspiring everyone within the school to believe in the ability of all students to achieve at high levels. These principals work explicitly and relentlessly to raise expectations throughout their school, ensuring that all students are improving and being held to high standards.

This climate of shared accountability is integral to ensuring that the entire school community moves forward toward achieving their vision of excellence for students. As we heard from Jackson, a shared vision and the conviction that all students can achieve at high levels, as well as a commitment to ensuring all voices are heard in shaping that vision, can lead to inspiring achievement and success for all students.

From the Noble Network of Charter Schools, we saw a leader who was relentlessly focused on "staffing up" his school and creating a "dream team" while also fostering a culture that valued and retained those top educators. Robinson's experience reflects the impact of a principal who openly shares how much time he spends on recruiting and selecting only the greatest teachers to ensure that every student in his school receives a high-quality education.

Education is, ultimately, people driven. Although innovation and technology will continue to enhance our ability to deliver exceptional learning opportunities, in the end it is the teacher in the classroom and the team within a school that makes learning possible. Our research shows that principals who focus on staffing up define selection criteria for whom they want to hire, setting a high bar for the characteristics they're seeking. They are most interested in applicants who show strong content knowledge and pedagogy, who bring a deep commitment to the belief that every student can achieve academic success, and who are seeking opportunities to learn and improve and want to work with teams.

A focus on staffing up also includes the intentional recruitment of the right candidates for openings. Beyond the hiring process, these principals are also quite deliberate about how they assign teachers to teams and students. They consistently look for ways to create strong grade-level or department teams of teachers with a range of experiences, and they ensure that their most effective teachers are serving the students in greatest need.

At the core intersection of the three major categories, and the underlying current of the three teacher perspectives in this chapter, is "cultivating leadership." Great principals clearly have a significant impact on student achievement, but principals can't do it alone—they need great leaders throughout their staff to drive change. That's why the most successful principals focus on cultivating staff leadership skills and encouraging the professional growth of teachers and other staff. By cultivating leadership skills early and often, mentoring school leaders, creating and fostering an Instructional Leadership Team, giving teachers a voice in decisions, and rewarding teachers with increased leadership opportunities, the highly effective principals we studied empowered their staff to be the driving force of change so that increasing effectiveness was the critical component of their school culture.

Throughout these teachers' discussions, the power and importance of developing leadership beyond the principal role was emphasized. Frieze, at E. L. Haynes, spoke to the importance of dialogue between school leaders and teachers "that encourages equity of voice and a sense of ownership and empowerment for everyone on staff." Jackson at Manning Elementary noted how impactful it was that her principal "allowed each teacher team to develop the best model to meet the needs of its particular students . . . When it comes to the school's budget, staffing, resource allocations, curriculum implementation, and more, our principal reaches out to teachers for solutions."

It is critical that principals do everything in their power to create clear pathways for effective teachers to expand their reach both inside and outside the classroom. Increased leadership opportunities allow teachers to continue to receive the support and development they need to improve their own effectiveness while also gaining opportunities to share those skills and practices with their school community, thus improving instructional effectiveness in many classrooms. These opportunities for leadership also lead to higher retention rates for teachers, as they experience real career growth and the ability to expand their impact.

This work is far from easy. Across the country, new policies and expectations for principals are responding to research findings by increasing the focus on instructional leadership and improving teacher effectiveness. At the same time, principals remain accountable for all aspects of general building management and operations. Yet, the most successful principals know how to prioritize their work and maintain a focus on what is most critical—ensuring that every teacher in every classroom in the school is supported and growing in his or her instructional effectiveness.

Teachers should be demanding this level of support from both their own school communities and their districts and states as well. With increased rigor and focus on principal preparation and evaluation programs, states and districts can ensure that principals have the necessary skills to continuously increase teacher effectiveness. This will also allow schools to continue to develop great teams of teachers and to provide pathways to leadership for those who express the interest and have the skills to be successful.

Through our work at New Leaders, we've been able to clearly identify these several actions as the most critical for principals to take in order to achieve success in supporting students to ever higher levels of achievement. As districts and states take on the development and implementation of new principal evaluations, we recommend that they use these practices—and their outcomes for teacher quality and retention—as the core of those evaluation systems. Namely:

- Principal evaluations should still place significant weight on student outcomes, as that is the end goal of our work in schools.
- From there, a large portion of the evaluation should focus on how well principals implement the key practices we've identified: developing teachers, managing talent, and creating a great place to work.
- As do teachers, principals need a clear understanding of what good practice in these areas looks like, and they need regular feedback about how well they implement these practices.
- Input from school staff—usually through teacher surveys—is crucial formative feedback for principals, as well as important evidence for evaluators to use in their ratings of principal practice.
- Although it is a challenging undertaking, we also look to states and districts to pilot the inclusion of measures around teacher effectiveness and retention of effective teachers in their principal evaluation models.

Frieze, Jackson, and Robinson spoke to the importance of strong, trusting relationships between teachers and school leaders to attract and retain the great teachers who will push their students to the highest levels of success. Now it is up to school systems to ensure that they develop policies and practices that prepare, hire, and evaluate principals against the key actions that attract, develop, and retain great teachers.

Students deserve the greatest teachers possible in their classrooms—not just in one classroom one year, but in every classroom they enter every year. Principals have the unique opportunity and responsibility to ensure this level of quality of instruction across our schools. Investing in principal quality—and raising our expectations around the principal role—is one of the strongest commitments we can make to maximizing teacher quality at scale.

7

Raising the Status of the Profession

FRAMING THE ISSUE

Edward Liu

Recent headlines, public rhetoric, and legislative actions once again highlight the ambiguous position teachers hold in U.S. society. On the one hand, teachers are lauded for their important work. Policy makers, politicians, and researchers all repeat the refrain that teachers are the most important school-based factor in determining the academic success of children, and they praise teachers' work as vital to the nation's future. At the same time, some of these same individuals are advancing policies that seek to regulate teachers' work more tightly, curtail their collective bargaining rights, abolish tenure and other job protections, or even publicly report estimates of their individual effectiveness in raising students' standardized test scores. In the public square, teachers are being simultaneously praised and disparaged; told their expertise is essential, but largely disregarded when it comes to ideas about how to improve education. In the workplace, teachers face a similarly ambiguous and confusing context. Many schools and districts are creating new, differentiated roles for teachers that provide them with leadership and growth opportunities, as well as recognition. At the same time, many teachers feel subject to increased control and scrutiny. They feel a loss of professional autonomy and trust in their judgment.

One thing that is clear, however, is that teacher quality has risen to the top of the education reform agenda. Ongoing policy debates about how to recruit and retain talented individuals for the teaching profession have tended to focus rightly on such matters as preservice and in-service preparation, entry and certification requirements, teacher evaluation and accountability, career ladders and differentiated roles, and salary and incentives. Largely ignored, however, has been the broader issue of the social status of the teaching profession and the impact of public regard (or the lack of it) on the teaching force. Status is a powerful extrinsic reward and can influence career decisions in complex ways. Without considering the impact that the social standing of teachers has on who enters the profession, how teachers feel about their work, and who stays in the profession, policy makers may end up crafting policies that fail to get the results they intend. One big policy puzzle is how to raise the status and social standing of K–12 teachers in the United States so that we can attract and keep the talent we need to meet the unprecedented goals we now have for public education. This is the puzzle that organizations like Teach Plus are trying to solve.

THE STATUS OF TEACHING AND TEACHERS

Sociologist Dan Lortie aptly described teaching as having middling status in the United States. As he pointed out almost four decades ago in *Schoolteacher*, a seminal work that remains salient today, teaching is *respectable* work, if not always highly respected.[1] It is a white-collar occupation that requires a bachelor's degree, and for much of U.S. history, schoolteachers have enjoyed a certain respect in their local communities. Most Americans agree that the work of educating youth is an important and worthwhile pursuit. Indeed, according to the forty-third annual Phi Delta Kappa/Gallup Poll, "three of four Americans support recruiting high-achieving high school students to become teachers, and . . . Two of three Americans would like a child of theirs to become a public school teacher."[2] At the same time, K–12 teaching is a very common profession, with over three million members—compared to approximately 730,000 lawyers and 690,000 physicians and surgeons[3]—and teaching has never enjoyed the status and respect in the United States that it has had in many other countries.

As Lortie noted, teaching is respectable but common, honored but disdained, praised but seen as easy work (with short days and summers off), considered a profession but also characterized by modest pay and high levels of unionization. This ambiguous status of teachers has long roots in U.S. history. Prior to the mid-twentieth century, teaching was largely a short-term occupation. It started as a predominantly male profession—as temporary work that men did on the way to joining the clergy or another higher-status occupation.[4] In the late nineteenth century, with the rise of public education and the move toward mass schooling, school systems turned to women as a source of labor, and K–12 teaching became a predominantly female profession. Many have argued that teaching's long association with "women's work" has contributed to its low status. Other historically female-dominated professions (or "pink-collar professions"), such as nursing, have also suffered from relatively low status and pay, despite requiring high levels of education and expertise.

Elementary and secondary school teaching has also long been subordinate to other related professions. As was mentioned, teaching was once largely a stepping stone to joining the clergy. Later, in the early twentieth century, K–12 teachers were relegated to a lower status in the educational field with the rise of a professional class of school administrators and the higher-education professoriate. School administrators and professors became high-profile spokespersons in the education field, and a pattern emerged in which individuals outside of the ranks of teachers became seen as experts above actual practitioners.[5] Here, too, gender likely played a role, as K–12 administrators and the professoriate were almost entirely male.

Another reason for teaching's relatively low prestige is that the profession has had a hard time claiming authority based on unique expertise. In part, this is because teaching is so common, and most U.S. citizens have had many years of long-term contact with teachers in their lives as students. As a result, teaching does not seem at all mysterious or special. Everyone knows many teachers and has been taught by them for years at a time. This points to the imperative of having a clear set of standards for the skills, knowledge, and dispositions teachers must bring to their classrooms and upon which teachers can claim unique authority over the challenges of their profession.

RAISING THE STATUS OF TEACHING

Although it is clear that we need to raise the status of teaching, how to do so is not obvious. What kinds of programs and policies will not only elevate the public's perception of teachers, but also make teaching a desirable field for ambitious high performers to both enter and stay in? What can we learn from nations that hold teachers in higher esteem, and how can these lessons be applied in ways that make sense in our American context? And where are we seeing pockets of work that are succeeding in these efforts and can potentially be replicated at scale?

EDUCATION LIBRARY
UNIVERSITY OF KENTUCKY

REFORMING TEACHER ENTRY AND TRAINING

Shouldn't We Hold Teachers (Like Me) to a Higher Standard?

Meaghan Petersack

In my fourth year teaching elementary school in Washington, DC, I left class early one day to attend a Capitol Hill meeting on higher education policy. One moment I was gathered with my students on our class carpet; the next, I found myself seated in the office of a long-time congressman. The carpet was plush blue and the walls were lined with etchings of some of the most important moments in our nation's history. I settled into a high-backed leather chair, relishing the opportunity to meet in this majestic setting with such a powerful individual.

The topic may have been education, but I wasn't there as a teacher. Even though I had been out of college for only a few years, I was lucky enough to serve in a young alumni position on the board of trustees for my Ivy League university. Our trustee group consisted of doctors, lawyers, bankers, journalists, and many other prestigious professionals. I was the only teacher in attendance.

A trustee began the informal gathering by asking the congressman about his daughter, who was also an alumna of our university. The congressman sighed heavily and said, "I guess she's doing well. I'm not sure she's really using her degree, though. She's a kindergarten teacher." My jaw dropped and the eyes of the other trustees in the room glanced uncomfortably in my direction. Before the tension in the room could build any higher, the university president gave me a quick smile and said, "Senator, we absolutely think that she is using her degree to the fullest potential. We are very proud of your daughter."

I was grateful for the president's defense of my profession and have been inspired by many like her, who acknowledge that teaching is an important and challenging job. But I walked away from that meeting believing that true education reform will not be possible without a seismic shift in the public perception of the teaching profession.

I believe that one of the best ways to elevate the teaching profession is to start at the beginning, with entry and training requirements. Beyond earning a bachelor's degree, there are currently few hurdles to becoming a teacher. With such a low bar for entry, it is difficult for teaching to be seen by the public as a prestigious profession. We have a deep respect for doctors and lawyers partly because we know they have undergone rigorous selection and training.

Looking back on my own entrance into the teaching profession, I wish I had been held to higher standards before taking on the deeply important responsibility of educating students. I entered the profession through Teach for America, a fast-track to teaching in urban schools. I did not complete any teaching coursework while in college, but this did not prevent me from passing the minimal requirements needed for a provisional teaching license in DC.

The first step in my journey to becoming a licensed teacher was passing a series of Praxis teaching exams. Friends and Teach for America staff members told me that I did not need to prepare in advance for these tests, as they covered basic elementary school skills and knowledge. Heeding their advice, I did absolutely no prep work or practice tests. About a month after taking it, I received a "Certificate of Excellence" for my high score on the exam. I then completed a five-week summer training program where I instructed a small group of students. While those weeks of training were intense, I ultimately received positive feedback from my coaches and was feeling optimistic about my potential as a classroom teacher.

I wish I could say that my strong performances on the Praxis tests and as a teacher-in-training were predictive of my success as a classroom teacher just weeks later. Unfortunately for my kindergarten students that first year, I was woefully unprepared to be a teacher. The gaps in my skills and knowledge prevented me from providing the high-quality early education that they needed and deserved. Now in my fifth year of teaching, I often think back to that first year, wishing I could go back in time armed with all the knowledge I have gained about young children and how they learn.

In 2012 the American Federation of Teachers (AFT) outlined a set of proposals to make teaching a more selective and highly trained profession.[6] The first of these proposals is to require passage of a comprehensive "bar exam" that covers a broad range of pedagogical and content knowledge. As someone who did well on one of the current entrance exams but did not feel prepared to teach, I think that a much more rigorous entrance exam would ensure a higher level of preparation for those entering the teaching profession.

Using a bar exam to measure preparedness would also hold schools of education and alternative certification programs to higher standards. In order to ensure that their graduates pass, many of these programs would need to change both the content and rigor of their course requirements. Looking back on my own preparation experience, I wish that I had been pushed to develop a solid understanding of child development and pedagogy for students in the first years of elementary education. I had exposure to such content knowledge in those five weeks of training, but I was never expected to show the kind of mastery that would make a difference in my practice as a first-year teacher.

While I think that requiring teachers to pass a bar exam is a step in the right direction, no single assessment can accurately capture all of the skills and knowledge that contribute to effective teaching. This is especially true of the "softer skills" required to invest students in learning, respond to their social and emotional needs, and create a positive and productive learning environment. Perhaps more so than other prestigious professions, teaching requires as much interpersonal skill as it does technical expertise. Therefore, reform of teacher preparation must also include some standards for competency in these domains—and one way to achieve this is to institute a mandatory residency year for teachers-in-training.

Most of the first- through third-year teachers surveyed by the AFT reported that they felt unprepared for the "realities" of classroom teaching, namely managing a large group of students and meeting their individual needs. In reaction to these findings, the AFT recommends that all teachers complete a full year of residency before entering the profession. I do not think you could find a current classroom teacher who thinks they would not have benefited tremendously from more on-the-job practice. During my summer training, I found it helpful to observe master teachers in action before trying a practice on my own. However, there are so many different techniques that teachers use throughout an entire school year that my short residency prevented me from having the complete toolkit I needed to succeed with my first class of kindergartners. Just as those entering the medical profession complete an intensive multiyear residency, there should be a higher standard for on-the-job practice for teachers, in which they assume increasing (and ultimately full) responsibility for students' education.

Raising the standards for teacher preparation programs is critical, but so too is ensuring that the students who enter those programs are of the highest possible caliber. The AFT suggests setting a minimum undergraduate grade point average for acceptance into a teacher preparation program. Research shows that the United States draws much of its teaching force from the bottom third of college graduates.[7] As a Teach for America alum, I do not always agree with the program's teacher selection and development theories, but I do appreciate that TFA has reversed this pattern for its applicants. And high entry requirements shouldn't be the purview of alternative certification programs only: surely schools of education could also attract stronger candidates, and filter out those who might struggle to meet the demands of teaching later on, by implementing more rigorous entry requirements and then providing a higher-quality, more intensive training program for accepted applicants.

As a fifth-year teacher who anticipates a long career in the profession, I would love to see the next generation of teachers reach higher standards of theory and practice before leading a classroom. If carefully designed and implemented, higher entry requirements for teacher preparation programs, a professional certification exam, and a mandatory year of residency have the potential to both significantly improve teacher quality and raise the public perception of the teaching profession.

Teachers make all other professions possible, and therefore we are every bit as vital to the health of our society as doctors. If we are to be respected as such, we need a route to teaching that expects the best of us, so that we can give the best to our students.

NOT MY PARENTS' PROFESSION

Today's Teachers Need Career Ladders

Erin Dukeshire

As the daughter of two educators, I grew up wanting to be a teacher. Dinner conversations in my family revolved around my mother's excitement over a new novel her class was reading and my father's systematic attempts to support his most troubled students. Fascinated, I imagined myself in their roles. I seemed to inherit their love of working with children, and I was drawn to the constant problem solving required for their career.

A generation after they entered the classroom, I stood in front of my first class in Homestead, Florida. Forty ninth graders sat crowded around small tables in a corner science lab without working air conditioners. Mo heckled hilariously from the back of the room, and Salvador pumped his fists in the air each time he earned an A. I delighted in getting to know these awesome students and in their eagerness to engage in a good lesson. At the same time, I was faced with the problem-solving opportunities I expected from the job. My students' academic and behavioral struggles constantly challenged me. My nights were spent planning lessons and conceiving of strategies to draw Calvin's eyes from his lap and prevent Tyana from storming out of the room. Challenged greatly during my first years of teaching, I committed to becoming the skilled teacher my students deserved—the kind of teachers I'd seen in my parents.

I returned home to Massachusetts and spent the next years furiously developing my craft. By my fifth year, thanks to coaching and opportunities to observe excellent colleagues, my classroom had become a source of pride for me and my students. Each of my adolescent scientists could generate unique, testable hypotheses, and their curious experimenting led to masterful explanations of subjects from electricity to the rock cycle. That year, my students flipped the achievement gap: a higher percentage of my predominantly low-income, minority students scored proficient on the state science exam than in the average Massachusetts school.

But I sat down in class one day, amidst my engaged fifth graders, and thought, "Is this all there is to teaching?"

I adored my students and the daily work, but leading a classroom no longer felt like enough to sustain me through an entire career. Though I'd seen several of my own fantastic teachers remain engaged in their careers by continuously improving their teaching practices, my goals were different.

The joys and compelling challenges of classroom teaching were not the only factors that brought me to the classroom. Ultimately, I decided to teach because I wanted to combat the unacceptably inequitable access of low-income and minority students to high-quality science education. I aimed to have an impact on more than the hundred students in my classes each day.

I also craved new ways to challenge myself professionally. I knew that I would always continue to improve my skills as a classroom teacher, but I also wondered about the new learning required to implement schoolwide change. My students would benefit from explicit connections between science and other content areas, as well as from their science teachers' deliberate planning to tie one grade's content to the learning from previous grades. Leading these changes across classes and grade levels seemed like difficult work, and I wanted to figure out how to do it well. Unfortunately, limited time and authority posed barriers to tackling these new goals. Seeing no room to expand my impact or develop diversified skills, I began to research other jobs.

Half of all urban teachers leave the classroom after three years. I'd made it to five, but that was almost it. Then, just as I was considering an exit from teaching, I stumbled upon several opportunities that provided the new challenges and greater impact I sought, without taking me out of the classroom.

At the time, a few Boston schools were recruiting cohorts of "teacher leaders" to lead school turnaround efforts. Rather than leave the profession, I was hired as a Turnaround Teacher Team (T3) teacher leader. Teaching science is still the most joyful aspect of my day, but developing the skills to mentor adults and facilitate schoolwide change is refreshing and satisfying (see chapter 2 for more on T3).

Additionally, my recommitment to classroom teaching has been supported by opportunities to impact policies that affect my students. As a Teach Plus Teaching Policy Fellow and America Achieves Fellow, I have had opportunities to provide feedback to policy makers about what works in my school and classroom, while relying upon expertise from my daily work with students.

I was lucky to have stumbled upon a handful of opportunities that have allowed me to contribute to solutions in the field of education without leaving the classroom. Differentiated leadership roles like mine are standard in some of our country's most respected professions. Practitioners of medicine, law, and business are rewarded for accomplishments with increased responsibility, and they are trusted to drive change in their own professions. Rarely are teachers provided with similar opportunities to serve as experts in their own field.

Providing my colleagues and me with decision-making opportunities common to other professions is not just a move to benefit the adults who seek broader impact; it's a key lever in improving results for kids. When effective teachers are respected as leaders, we contribute to solutions throughout our schools, districts, and beyond while continuing to work directly with our own students. Our decisions are driven by knowledge of these children and what works in our classrooms. My school, which instituted the T3 Initiative at the start of its school turnaround process, has improved student growth from among the worst in the state to among the best. Recruiting and empowering effective teachers through formalized hybrid leadership roles has been important to our students' success.

All great teachers are ambitious, like effective practitioners of any profession. The teaching profession is currently designed to retain the many excellent teachers whose ambition remains focused on best serving the students they directly teach. But other teachers have goals, like I do, that are more divided—we want to tackle diverse professional challenges and to have an impact both on our own students and on their peers beyond our classrooms.

When my mother sought schoolwide impact and compensation for her work, becoming an administrator was her only option. If my situation were the same, I would no longer be teaching. Hybrid roles that are compensated and based on demonstrated efficacy can keep us in the profession. Districts must make such career paths the norm to keep classrooms full of the great teachers our students deserve.

TOO SMART TO BE A TEACHER?

Let's Prove My Grandmother Wrong

Jaime Siebrase Hudgins

Whenever I see my grandmother, I am met with the question, "Have you decided to go to law school yet?" My response is always, "No, I love teaching." After an awkward silence and a deep sigh, Grandma advises me that I am wasting my talents and education by teaching. "You," she says, "are too smart to be a teacher."

Throughout my career, I have encountered individuals just like Grandma—those who believe that teaching is a career path for the unable and unmotivated, not for well-educated, successful, ambitious professionals. Herein lies a critical problem with the teaching profession in the United States—and consequently with the state of education: teachers are not accorded the same status as other highly skilled professionals. How do we fight the "Grandma mentality" and encourage our nation's brightest students to consider education as a career? By changing how we recruit, train, and compensate teachers.

Teacher recruitment in the United States differs greatly from that in top-performing nations like Singapore and Finland. In these countries, teachers are required to undergo a rigorous selection process with stringent requirements. For instance, Singaporean candidates are required to be in the top 30 percent of their undergraduate classes. In Finland, prospective teachers should be in the top 20 percent. Candidates in both nations are required to pass extensive exams that test literacy, numeracy, and problem solving before becoming eligible to attend teacher preparation programs. Interviews for these programs generally require candidates to complete performance tasks for a panel of experienced educators to determine their aptitude and suitability for a teaching career. In Singapore, only 20 percent of candidates with qualifying scores are accepted to teacher education programs. Finnish candidates have a 10 percent chance of being accepted.[8] Essentially, only those with outstanding academic achievement and demonstrated competency in areas associated with successful teaching are allowed to enter teacher preparation programs. How can the United States replicate this achievement?

We need to attract our nation's top undergraduates to a career that is challenging, rewarding, and respected. Selective teacher fellowships and residency programs send only a small percentage of all new educators into classrooms, and ultimately serve as a limited fast track for entry into the profession without addressing the overall quality of teacher selection and preparation, particularly in comparison with international leaders. Policy makers should consider adopting the recruitment and selection strategies of these highly selective nations and organizations to determine entry into the profession for all new teachers. If selection into a teaching program were as competitive and rigorous as that for law or medical school, more top students might be interested, and the status of the profession would inevitably improve.

Such a shift would be a giant step toward recruiting promising recent graduates to the profession, but reforms must also include an often-ignored source of top talent: career changers. I did not enter the teaching profession via a traditional path. In fact, my undergraduate institution did not offer education as an undergraduate major. Like most of my peers in my graduating class, I was set on graduate school (maybe even law school, but don't tell Grandma) and a fast-paced, rewarding career. I envisioned working toward my next promotion, glossy business cards, and having the financial means to jet off to the Dominican Republic for an extended weekend. Before I entered teaching, I spent a few years in corporate America, working for a publishing company, and then completed a graduate degree in history. My intuition told me that teaching would be a rewarding career, but even I fell victim to the general perception of the profession. I thought to myself, "I have two degrees. Why would I want to teach when I could work 9 to 5 with great pay and benefits, and go shopping on my lunch break?"

But as it turns out, life in cubicle land wasn't all that exciting. I longed to use my love of learning in a meaningful way. I made the momentous decision to move to a new city and become a teacher. What I did not anticipate was how difficult the transition would be, due partly to my own preconceived notions about teaching ("really, how hard can it be?") and partly to the difficulty of landing a teaching job. Recruitment and licensure processes favor newly minted undergraduate education graduates, making it difficult for a career changer like me to enter the profession. I had a bachelor's and a master's degree in the subjects I wanted to teach and outstanding scores on the teacher content exam, but I could not find a teaching job. I turned to an urban school district with a teacher shortage substantial enough that I could be hired and granted an "alternative" license, as long as I completed the required coursework within three years. Though many principals wanted teachers with full licensure, I was able to persuade one to take a chance on me. Despite that principal's belief that I wouldn't make it to Christmas break, I stayed at that school for five years, and though I've since moved, I'm still in the classroom.

In addition to attracting the top undergraduates, policies need to be created that provide options for nontraditional candidates to enter the profession. Alternatively licensed teachers can be equally successful as those who enter the profession via a traditional undergraduate education program. By not providing widespread, supportive programs that help transition these individuals into the classroom, we might be neglecting a potentially incredible talent pool.

Changes in the recruitment and selection of future teachers would be meaningless without a significant change in the quality of teacher education programs. Even though I took a nontraditional path into teaching, I do believe that quality training in pedagogy and hands-on preparation is essential to classroom success. I spent two and a half years completing the required courses to gain full, professional licensure in my state. At the time, I was in my first years teaching and desperate to learn strategies and methods that I could implement in my classroom. I wanted to know how to teach high-school-level material to students who were reading significantly below grade level and manage a classroom of thirty-five teenagers who, like my principal, anticipated my pre–Christmas break departure. My experience taking education courses at the local university, the top supplier of teachers for my district, was horrifying. The coursework lacked rigor, my classmates were the poster children for the unable and unmotivated teacher stereotype, and, most disappointingly, the courses offered were lacking in any real classroom application. Classes focusing on the history of education in the United States, while appealing to me as a historian, did not provide me with the strategies and skills needed to successfully teach my students.

Schools of education should work collectively with their local school districts to prepare their graduates for classroom excellence. This collaboration should include the adoption of residency programs where new teachers are placed with mentor teachers with proven records of success, complete a yearlong classroom placement, and receive continuous feedback. A critical difference between this model and the more standard "student teacher" model is that during the residency period, the new teacher is an employee of the school district as well as a student in the teacher preparation program, thus receiving compensation in the form of a stipend or salary. This would ease the financial burden that may discourage some career changers from entering the profession. If more districts adopted a residency model, new teachers would be assured a valuable, mentor-supported classroom experience as paid professionals while simultaneously enrolled as students to learn the pedagogical methods crucial to classroom success.

Another critically necessary structural change in our nation's teacher training programs is greater accountability for schools of education based on the performance of their graduates. Unless the stakes are raised for education schools and their graduates, the status quo of mediocre preparation will continue to prevail for the vast majority of programs.

The political climate is currently ripe for this type of change. Recently, the U.S. Department of Education announced a proposal to increase the accountability of education schools through grants to states that identify top performing schools of education and alternative route programs and provide scholarships for such programs.[9] Implementation of this level of oversight could force teacher preparation programs to become more selective. The increased competition for admittance and the opening of alternative paths that do not currently exist could remove the stigma of the assumption present on many college campuses that students choose to enter education because they failed to gain entrance to a more rigorous profession. When being admitted to your college's school of education is as competitive as the school of engineering or medicine, more high-achieving potential teachers will take note, and the perception of the teaching profession will improve dramatically for the next generation of educators.

No discussion of raising the status of the teaching profession can ignore the question of compensation. For talented individuals to be attracted to a profession, they must know that they will be treated, and compensated, as professionals. One of the most common misconceptions about teachers is that we enter the field for the short workday and the long summer break.

I am dedicated to my profession and my students, but no more so than many colleagues at my school. This school year, I've averaged about 70 hours per week doing the work I need to do to perform my teaching duties—time that does not include professional development and other professional opportunities. At my current salary level, this is roughly $17.46 per hour. And those lengthy summer breaks? Those open up time for conferences and professional development, for which teachers often absorb the cost.

Teaching is a professional career that requires, at a bare minimum, an undergraduate degree and, like many other professions, continuous professional development. In order to raise the status of the teaching profession in the minds of the talented young graduates and career changers we want in our classrooms, we must offer compensation at levels comparable to lawyers, not their administrative assistants. This is a difficult task, especially when states and school districts across the nation are facing record budget shortfalls. But if we are serious about improving the status of the teaching profession by attracting top talent and, in turn, improving teacher effectiveness and student achievement, we must search for innovative ways to compensate our teachers as the professionals they are. The current model of compensation in many, if not most, districts nationwide rewards teachers only for longevity in the classroom and degrees—neither of which is necessarily the primary indicator of a teacher's success with students. Assuming that our most talented college graduates and career changers are driven individuals, why would they want to enter a profession where compensation is "one size fits most," with no reward for assuming additional responsibilities or achieving the most important goal, improving results for students?

There is no silver bullet that will cure the "Grandma mentality." But as the baby boom generation of educators approaches retirement, we have a unique opportunity to fill the void that they leave with the best new talent our nation has to offer—if comprehensive changes are undertaken to make teaching a great option. Then, and only then, will we begin to see a change in the perception and prestige of the teaching profession and the resulting improvement in our education system as a whole.

RESPONSE

Edward Liu

The teacher authors in this chapter present thoughtful and incisive ideas for raising the status of the teaching profession. Both Meaghan Petersack and Jaime Hudgins argue that strengthening the entry requirements and preparation of teachers would help increase the profession's prestige. In their own ways, both were disheartened by the relatively low rigor of the preparation programs they themselves experienced.

One reason for these low standards has been the teaching profession's lack of influence over preparation and certification standards, and the supply of teachers. In teaching, training and certification requirements are largely set by state governments rather than by members of the profession, as in law and medicine, where professional associations help to regulate the profession. Until recently, when teachers were in short supply in certain areas, it was common practice for states to grant emergency waivers to allow unlicensed candidates to teach. This willingness to suspend certification requirements reflected a belief that there is not much of a specialized knowledge or skills base that all teachers must have in order to practice. To many, strong academic preparation in subject matter and certain personal characteristics are what are essential rather than training in pedagogy, curriculum, human development, or clinical practice. Indeed, some policy analysts argue that one way to increase the supply of talent in the field would be to reduce the barriers to entry and simply use on-the-job performance to judge whether the individual ought to continue in the profession.[10] One has a hard time imagining the same arguments being proposed as a way to increase quality in other professions, such as medicine and law.

Petersack and Hudgins reject this line of reasoning. Although they both entered teaching through nontraditional routes, these now experienced and successful teachers argue for the importance of strong preparation for the challenging work teachers do. They separately suggest that the profession adopt a residency model in which teachers prepare to teach under the guidance of accomplished mentor teachers and only gradually assume full teaching responsibilities over an extended period of time. Teaching is one of the only professions in which novices are expected, on their first day, to do essentially the same job as thirty-year veterans. In part, this is why teaching is often perceived as simple and common: if a newcomer can walk into a classroom and be expected to do the same thing as a long-time practitioner, surely the skills required are not particularly demanding.

Yet commonness alone cannot explain why teachers do not enjoy the respect and esteem in the United States that they do in other nations. Citizens in other nations with universal schooling also have extended contact with teachers, and in these nations teaching is also one of the largest professions. However, in nations such as Japan, Finland, and Singapore, teachers are more highly respected and the profession holds more status than in the United States. In Finland, as Hudgins notes, teachers are recruited from the top 20 percent of the high school academic cohort, and "partly owing to its prestige, teaching is the most popular career choice and the most admired profession among top students, outpolling law and medicine."[11] East Asian nations are strongly influenced by Confucian thought tracing back to the sixth century BCE, which established a deep respect for teachers. In China, for instance, "the career hierarchy of K–12 teachers is comparable in prestige to that for higher education, and master teachers see themselves as being at the same level in the K–12 system as distinguished professors do at universities."[12] Teachers in China progress through a series of ranks from apprentice to second rank, first rank, senior rank, and a variety of "super" ranks. The expertise of accomplished teachers is recognized, and they are enlisted to mentor beginning teachers, review the lesson plans of novices or struggling veterans, teach demonstration lessons, lead lesson study, and contribute to the professional literature by publishing articles in teacher journals. In the prosperous provinces of China, then, teachers have what teacher-author Erin Dukeshire argues for: differentiated roles and a career ladder that does not remove them entirely from the classroom.

In her essay, Dukeshire describes how she reached a plateau in her fifth year of teaching and was hungry for new professional challenges. She was fortunate to encounter a number of teacher leadership opportunities, and these opportunities have sustained and kept her in teaching. The types of teacher leadership roles that Dukeshire argues can help increase the status of teaching have been proliferating rapidly over the past decade and a half. Yet there are several challenges to their taking root and becoming permanent parts of the U.S. education system. These challenges are both cultural—pertaining to strong norms of autonomy and egalitarianism in teaching[13]—and financial—pertaining to the failure of many districts to institutionalize and adequately fund and support these roles.[14] Too often, schools and districts implement teacher leadership positions as add-on roles—that is, roles that ask full-time classroom teachers to take on additional responsibilities on top of a full teaching load, or that make only minor adjustments to the teacher's schedule and teaching duties.[15] Many districts offer very modest stipends in exchange for what are, on paper, substantial new responsibilities. What relatively few schools and districts have done is to carefully think through how to change structures and devote resources (in the form of teacher release time, training, and compensation) to make these roles realistic, doable, desirable, and worthy of respect.

The authors in this chapter address two other strategies for raising the status of teaching: reforming pay and improving recruitment. As Hudgins points out, "No discussion of raising the status of the teaching profession can ignore the question of compensation. For talented individuals to be attracted to a profession, they must know that they will be treated, and compensated, as professionals." In a culture where status is quite strongly associated with income, this seems like common sense. Yet, the relationship between pay and status is complicated. One can think of many examples of occupations that pay as much as or more than teaching but have lower status; and others, such as college teaching, that have higher status but similar pay. Moreover, as Hudgins acknowledges, in the short to medium term, with state and federal budgets under strain, one has a hard time seeing across-the-board raises in teacher pay, though it might be possible to change the structure of pay without necessarily increasing the overall amount spent.

There is certainly no shortage of proposals for how to restructure teacher pay, and some of the more dramatic proposals are quite controversial both within and outside the profession. Even if the field does not make any dramatic changes to the single-salary schedule, one could imagine, as a first step, at least setting more reasonable stipend levels for the teacher leadership roles Dukeshire describes. As a field, we send mixed messages when we tell teachers, "We have this challenging and important teacher leadership role that you should consider applying for and devoting your energy to, but we're only going to pay you a $700 stipend for the entire year for taking on this work." A true career ladder might offer somewhat lower starting salaries for new teachers who are part of a residency program in which they are still preparing to become teachers and aren't yet carrying a full teaching load, and somewhat higher salaries/stipends for those teachers who are carrying various teacher leadership roles, including helping these novice teachers develop. This is similar to what happens in medicine, where interns and residents are paid less than full-fledged doctors while they learn their craft under the supervision of attending physicians.

Another strategy for raising the status of the teaching profession involves aggressively targeting graduates from elite universities and making teaching an attractive option in these high-status institutions. Petersack mentions that the broader education field can learn from Teach for America's success in recruiting talent. Teach for America has been extraordinarily successful in recruiting some of the nation's most talented college graduates into teaching for at least two years. Yet the impact of Teach for America on the broader status of teaching is unclear. On the one hand, it has certainly established teaching as a worthwhile pursuit for the country's "best and brightest"—at least for a short time (the commitment requires two years). In the organization's literature, it reframes teaching as leadership, and argues that teaching in a high-need classroom develops leadership, planning, and organizational skills that are valuable in other sectors. This is a powerful counternarrative to the "those who can't, teach" saying. However, it may well be that Teach for America has developed a high-status credential for its corps members, but is having minimal impact on the broader status of the profession as a whole. Moreover, some have argued that Teach for America—by fast-tracking corps members into classrooms after a five-week intensive training period—reduces the overall status of teaching by reinforcing the view that there is no (or a very limited) knowledge or skill base that all teachers need to have before working with children.

The individual strategies discussed and proposed by the authors of this chapter—raising and/or restructuring teacher pay, aggressively recruiting talented individuals to join the profession, raising entry standards, improving the rigor and relevance of teacher preparation, creating differentiated roles and building a career ladder for teachers—are all sensible. Yet, I suspect that, in addition to trying to implement these technical fixes to the profession, we need to somehow find a way to tackle the underlying cultural beliefs that are holding down the status of the teaching profession. At the heart of the problem are: (1) the belief, on the part of too many Americans, that teaching is not all that hard, and (2) a failure to understand or appreciate what it means to actually try to achieve the goal of educating all children to high levels. Changing these beliefs, which have strong historical and cultural roots, will not be easy. One thing that may make a difference, however, is for more teachers to begin to publicly voice their experiences and their ideas for improving education—to more vigorously assert their expertise in the policy debates that affect them and the students they serve. With more teachers speaking out about the challenges they face and proposing possible solutions for some of these challenges, the public may finally begin to view them as what they are: highly skilled practitioners in an incredibly complex line of work.

CONCLUSION

Where Do We Go from Here?—Turning Teacher Voice into Action

Kate McGovern

In politics, everyone loves a teacher. When teachers popped up in the 2012 presidential debate on foreign policy, moderator and journalist Bob Schieffer interjected, "I think we *all* love teachers," in an effort to bring the discussion back to something more controversial. His almost exasperated tone suggested that this was basically a foregone conclusion: of course everyone loves teachers. The education wonks on Twitter went wild—*shout-out to teachers!*—but in the real world, a cursory nod of approval for teachers is neither sufficient nor a given. In practice, teachers are just as often blamed for their shortcomings as they are applauded for their daily work.

This book points to a more nuanced reality of public education today: that neither unconditional, patronizing affection for teachers, nor unreasonable criticism of them will solve the challenges facing our schools. Neither will provide all children with access to the kind of exciting, rigorous learning opportunities that they deserve. To do that—to transform our education system so that it best serves all students—we need to prioritize teachers' voices and the solutions their voices are raising.

At Teach Plus, I have the great privilege of spending much of my time listening to teachers' stories. I don't mean nice stories about how much they love their students, although they invariably do, or litanies of complaints about red tape and incompetency in their districts or administrations, although those crop up, too. Rather, I mean stories of how policies that are often enacted and implemented without teachers' input affect their classrooms—and what kinds of policies and implementation strategies they think would make schools better. There is great urgency in these stories: these teachers want every child in their classrooms to succeed; they want to see positive change today, not years from now, and they have ideas for how to make it happen.

In this book, you've seen just the tip of the teacher-driven-solutions iceberg. Stephanie Widmer advocates for school cultures that prioritize collaboration and ongoing structures for feedback. Sujata Bhatt is using data to invest her students in their learning. Erin Dukeshire and Lisa Goncalves show us that when you let teachers design shared leadership structures, incredible school change is possible. Jeremy Robinson tells us what principals need to do to keep their best teachers. And the teachers whose voices are represented here are not so different from many of their colleagues. Across the country, talented, passionate educators seek opportunities to be the problem solvers of their profession, to tackle challenges both within and beyond their classrooms, and to share their stories with policy makers, school and district leaders, and the general public.

But those stories alone are not enough. It is undoubtedly important that teachers' real, on-the-ground experiences are heard by the people who set the policies that affect their classrooms. But if we want to see real change in our struggling schools, sustainable excellence in our thriving ones, and a profession that recruits and retains top performers and treats them as the skilled professionals that they are, we must demand not only that teachers' stories are heard, but also that teachers themselves are engaged in the process of crafting and implementing education policies. Teacher voice must be translated into action. If the district, union, and nonprofit leaders in these pages are any indication, there is broad consensus that teachers' perspectives are critical—and such recognition in itself is a significant accomplishment of recent years. But avenues to engaging teachers in the process of transforming education remain less clear than the value of that engagement.

As we move forward with building a more effective, more equitable education system for children, it is not enough to give lip service to the importance of teacher voice. We must also be relentless in the pursuit of opportunities that put teachers at the table with policy makers, and then take those conversations and turn them into meaningful, sustainable change: evaluation systems that are built with teachers' direct input at multiple stages; unions that represent and advocate for the perspectives of both early career and veteran teachers; assessment protocols that use tests that teachers, not publishing houses, tell us are useful.

Many of the teachers in this book have found ways to push through existing barriers to effect change beyond their classrooms. But how do we open more avenues, so that direct teacher involvement in the policy process is the rule, not the exception? Across the country, there are isolated examples of formalized leadership roles that place teachers in positions of power and engagement with education policy. Current teachers, for example, can serve as Teaching Ambassador Fellows for the U.S. Department of Education, choosing to take either a one-year leave of absence from their classrooms to work full-time in the department, or to serve as part-time fellows in their local districts while continuing to teach. Some states, too, are moving toward formal advisory roles for current teachers. In Indiana, Tina Ahlgren served on the Indiana Department of Education's Education Reform Cabinet. These kinds of institutional roles for teachers should become the norm nationwide. Every local school board should have a current teacher on its roster; every state department of education should work with a teacher cabinet that plays an active role in advising state policy makers on what works best for teachers and kids. Our current model allows particularly scrappy teachers—some of whom you've heard from in this book—to be actively involved in changing education policy. But moving forward, we must push for the systemic inclusion of current teachers in formalized leadership roles at the local, state, and federal levels.

The teachers in these pages present a powerful argument for the possibilities of this work. They are the real experts: both skilled practitioners with great passion for providing their students with excellence every day, and creative problem solvers who are prepared not only to acknowledge the challenges of their field, but also to tackle them. It's time to let them.

NOTES

Introduction

1. National Center for Education Statistics. (2008). Schools and Staffing Survey. Washington, DC: National Center for Education Statistics, Institute of Education Sciences, http://nces.ed.gov/surveys/sass/tables/sass0708_011_t12n_02.asp.

2. Teoh, M. and Coggins, C. (2012). *Great Expectations: Teachers' Views on Elevating the Teaching Profession.* Boston: Teach Plus.

Chapter 1

1. Henrichson, C. and Delaney, R. (2012). *The Price of Prisons: What Incarceration Costs Taxpayers.* New York: Vera Institute of Justice, 10.

2. Education Week and Editorial Projects in Education Research Center. (2013). *Quality Counts 2013: Code of Conduct: Safety, Discipline and School Climate.* Bethesda, MD: Editorial Projects in Education.

3. Bill and Melinda Gates Foundation. (2013). *Ensuring Fair and Reliable Measures of Effective Teaching: Culminating Findings from the MET Project's Three-Year Study.* Seattle: Bill and Melinda Gates Foundation.

4. Jackson, K. (2013). *Non-Cognitive Ability, Test Scores, and Teacher Quality: Evidence from* 9th *Grade Teachers in North Carolina.* National Bureau of Economic Research, http://works.bepress.com/cgi/viewcontentcgi?article=1027&context=c_kirabo_jackson.

5. Wiener, R. and Lundy, K. (2013). *Evaluating Evaluations: Using Teacher Surveys to Strengthen Implementation*, Aspen Institute, http://www.aspeninstitute.org/publications/evaluating-evaluations-using-teacher-surveys-strengthen-implementation.

6. Bill and Melinda Gates Foundation, *Ensuring Fair and Reliable Measures of Effective Teaching.*

7. Bryk, A. S. and Schneider, B. (2004). *Trust in Schools: A Core Resource for Improvement.* New York: Russell Sage Foundation.

8. See Wiener and Lundy, *Evaluating Evaluations, supra* note 5, for description and discussion of the use of survey data in Aspire Public Schools.

9. McInnis, D. (Summer 2006). "What System?" *Dartmouth Medicine* 30, no. 2: 32.

Chapter 2

1. Almy, S. and Theokas, C. (2010). *Not Prepared for Class: High-Poverty Schools Continue to Have Fewer In-Field Teachers.* Washington, DC: The Education Trust.

2. Kalogrides, D., Loeb, S., and Beteille, T. (2011). *Power Play: Teacher Characteristics and Class Assignments.* Washington, DC: National Center for Analysis of Longitudinal Data in Education Research, The Urban Institute.

3. Tennessee Department of Education. (2007). "Tennessee's Most Effective Teachers," http://tennessee.gov/education/nclb/doc/TeacherEffectiveness2007_03.pdf.

4. Hahnel, C. and Jackson, O. (2012). *Learning Denied: The Case for Equitable Access in California's Largest School District.* Oakland, CA: The Education Trust–West.

5. Teach Plus. (2012). *Closing the Gap: Progress over Two Years in the T3 Initiative.* Boston: Teach Plus.

6. Johnson, S. M., Kraft, M. A., and Papay, J. P. (2012). "How Context Matters in High-Need Schools: The Effect of Teachers' Working Conditions on Their Professional Satisfaction and Their Students' Achievement," *Teachers College Record* 114, no. 10.

Chapter 3

1. Weisberg, D. et al. (2009). *The Widget Effect: Our National Failure to Acknowledge and Act on Differences in Teacher Effectiveness.* Brooklyn, NY: TNTP.

2. Hanushek, E. (2002). "Teacher Quality." In *Teacher Quality,* Lance T. Izumi and Williamson M. Evers (Eds.). Stanford, CA: Hoover Institution Press.

3. Weisberg et al. *The Widget Effect.*

4. Teoh, M. and Coggins, C. (2012). *Great Expectations: Teachers' Views on Elevating the Teaching Profession.* Boston: Teach Plus.

5. TNTP. (2012). *The Irreplaceables: Understanding the Real Retention Crisis in America's Urban Schools.* Brooklyn, NY: TNTP.

6. Memphis City Schools merged with the Shelby County School District in 2013.

7. The Bill and Melinda Gates Foundation (2013). *Ensuring Fair and Reliable Measures of Effective Teaching: Culminating Findings from the MET Project's Three-Year Study.* Seattle: Bill and Melinda Gates Foundation.

Chapter 4

1. Hanushek, E. (2002). "Teacher Quality." In *Teacher Quality,* Lance T. Izumi and Williamson M. Evers (Eds.). Stanford, CA: Hoover Institution Press.

2. Boyd, D. et al. (2010). *Teacher Layoffs: An Empirical Illustration of Seniority vs. Measures of Effectiveness.* Washington, DC: The Urban Institute.

3. Felch, J., Song, J., and Smith, D. "When Layoffs Come to L.A. Schools, Performance Doesn't Count," *Los Angeles Times,* December 4, 2010.

4. National Center for Education Statistics. (2008). Schools and Staffing Survey. Washington, DC: National Center for Education Statistics, Institute of Education Sciences, http://nces.ed.gov/surveys/sass/tables/sass0708_011_t12n_02.asp.

5. Los Angeles Unified School District, "Graduation and Dropout Rates," August 9, 2011, http://data.lausd.net/sites/data.lausd.net/files/Release%20of%20Grad%20and%20Dropout%20Stats%20Informative%208-9-11.pdf.

6. Blume, H. "LAUSD Weighs Lower Bar for Grads," *Los Angeles Times,* April 18, 2012.

7. Goldhaber, D. and Theobold, R. "Assessing the Determinants and Implications of Teacher Layoffs" (working paper no. 55, National Center for Analysis of Longitudinal Data in Education Research (CALDER), Washington, DC, 2010).

8. Bill and Melinda Gates Foundation. (2013). *Ensuring Fair and Reliable Measures of Effective Teaching: Culminating Findings from the MET Project's Three-Year Study.* Seattle: Bill and Melinda Gates Foundation.

9. Felch et al., "When Layoffs Come to L.A. Schools."

10. California Teachers Association. Press Release: "Prop. 30 Leads to Dramatic Drop in Educator Pink Slips—3,000 Issued Across State," March 18, 2013, http://www.cta.org/About-CTA/News-Room/Press-Releases/2013/03/20130318_1.aspx.

11. American Civil Liberties Union. (2011). "Judge Approves Landmark Settlement in Reed v. State of California," January 21, 2011, http://www.aclu-sc.org/judge-approves-landmark-settlement-in-reed-v-state-of-california/.

Chapter 5

1. National Center for Education Statistics. (2008). Schools and Staffing Survey. Washington, DC: National Center for Education Statistics, Institute of Education Sciences, http://nces.ed.gov/surveys/sass/tables/sass0708_011_t12n_02.asp.

2. Johnson, S. M. and Kardos, S. M. (2005). "Bridging the Generation Gap," *Educational Leadership* 62, no. 8.

3. "Rubber room" is the nickname used to refer to New York City's Temporary Reassignment Centers, where until recently teachers who had been removed from their classrooms were paid in full, sometimes for years, to await the arbitration processes required to remove them permanently from the school system. See Brill, S. "The Rubber Room," *New Yorker,* August 31, 2009.

4. Massachusetts continues to have a persistent achievement gap between students of color and their white classmates. While these gaps have narrowed between 1992 and 2011, we still have work to do. See Press Release: "Massachusetts Students Earn Top Scores on Nation's Report Card for Fourth Consecutive Exam Year," November 1, 2011, http://www.mass.gov/governor/pressoffice/pressreleases/2011/11111-naeps-results-released.html. Though unionization and high test scores are correlated in my state and several others, this isn't necessarily a causal relationship: other factors

could plausibly contribute; for example, the average education and income levels of residents in the state.

5. Farkas, S., Johnson, J., and Duffett, A. (2003). *Stand by Me: What Teachers Really Think about Unions, Merit Pay and Other Professional Matters.* New York: Public Agenda.

6. Silva, E. (2007). *On the Clock: Rethinking the Way Schools Use Time.* Washington, DC: Education Sector; Silva, E. (2012). *Off the Clock: What More Time Can (and Can't) Do for School Turnarounds.* Washington, DC: Education Sector; Kaplan, C. and Chan, R. (2011). *Time Well Spent: Eight Powerful Practices of Successful, Expanded-Time Schools.* Boston: National Center on Time and Learning.

7. Allensworth, E. (October 2006). Update to: *From High School to the Future: A First Look at Chicago Public School Graduates' College Enrollment, College Preparation, and Graduation from Four-Year Colleges.* Chicago: Consortium on Chicago School Research at the University of Chicago.

8. Rosenberg, S. and Silva, E. (2012). *Trending Toward Reform: Teachers Speak on Unions and the Future of the Profession.* Washington, DC: Education Sector; Teoh, M. and Coggins, C. (2012). *Great Expectations: Teachers' Views on Elevating the Teaching Profession.* Boston: Teach Plus.

9. Data collected from teachers at live Teach Plus Network event, November 9, 2010, http://www.teachplus.org/uploads/Documents/1293725888_20101109BostonEventData.pdf.

10. Massachusetts Teachers Association (2012). "Educator Evaluation Toolkit," http://www.massteacher.org/advocating/Evaluation.aspx.

Chapter 6

1. Leithwood, K. et al. (2004). *How Leadership Influences Student Learning.* New York: Wallace Foundation; Marzano, R., Waters, T., and McNulty, B. (2005). *School Leadership That Works: From Research to Results.* Alexandria, VA: Association for Supervision and Curriculum Development.

2. Marzano et al. *School Leadership That Works.*

3. Branch, G. F., Hanushek, E., and Rivkin, S. "Estimating the Effects of Leaders on Public Sector Productivity: The Case of School Principals" (working paper no. 17803, National Bureau of Economic Research, Cambridge, MA, 2012).

4. Scholastic and the Bill and Melinda Gates Foundation. (2010). *Primary Sources: America's Teachers on America's Schools.* New York: Scholastic.

5. TNTP. (2012). *The Irreplaceables: Understanding the Real Retention Crisis in America's Urban Schools.* Brooklyn, NY: TNTP.

6. Ibid.

7. Ronfeldt, M., Loeb, S., and Wyckoff, J. "How Teacher Turnover Harms Student Achievement" (working paper 70, National Center for Analysis of Longitudinal Data in Education Research, Washington, DC, 2012).

8. New Teacher Center, "Teaching and Learning Conditions Survey," http://www.newteachercenter.org/teaching-learning-conditions-survey.

9. TNTP, *The Irreplaceables.*

10. Ikemoto, G., Taliaferro, L., and Adams, E. (2012). *Playmakers: How Great Principals Build and Lead Great Teams of Teachers.* New York: New Leaders.

Chapter 7

1. Lortie, D. (1975). *Schoolteacher: A Sociological Perspective.* Chicago: The University of Chicago Press.

2. Bushaw, W. J. and Lopez, S. J. (2011). "Betting on Teachers: The 43rd Annual Phi Delta Kappa/Gallup Poll of the Public's Attitudes Toward the Public Schools," *Phi Delta Kappan* 93, no. 1: 10.

3. Bureau of Labor Statistics. "Occupational Outlook Handbook, 2012–13 Edition," http://www.bls.gov/ooh/.

4. Rury, J. L. (1989). "Who Became Teachers? The Social Characteristics of Teachers in American History," In *American Teachers: Histories of a Profession at Work,* D. Warren (Ed.). New York: McMillan, 7–48.

5. Lortie, *Schoolteacher.*

6. American Federation of Teachers Teacher Preparation Task Force. (2012). *Raising the Bar: Aligning and Elevating Teacher Preparation and the Teaching Profession.* Washington, DC: American Federation of Teachers.

7. Auguste, B., Kihn, P., and Miller, M. (2010). *Closing the Talent Gap: Attracting and Retaining Top-Third Graduates to Careers in Teaching: An International and Market Research-Based Perspective.* London: McKinsey & Company.

8. Barber, M. and Mourshed, M. (2007). *How the World's Best-Performing School Systems Come Out on Top.* London: McKinsey & Company.

9. U.S. Department of Education. (2011). *Our Future, Our Teachers: The Obama Administration's Plan for Teacher Education Reform and Improvement.* Washington, DC: U.S. Department of Education.

10. Gordon, R., Kane, T. J., and Staiger, D. O. (2006). *Identifying Effective Teachers Using Performance on the Job.* Washington, DC: Brookings Institution; Thomas B. Fordham Foundation. (1999). "The Teachers We Need and How to Get More of Them: A Manifesto." In *Better Teachers, Better Schools*, M. Kanstoroom and C. Finn, Jr. (Eds.). Washington, DC: Thomas B. Fordham Foundation, 1–18.

11. Auguste et al., *Closing the Talent Gap,* 19.

12. Ferreras, A. and Olson, S. (2010). *The Teacher Development Continuum in the United States and China: Summary of a Workshop*. Washington, DC: The National Academies Press.

13. Donaldson, M. L. et al. (2008). "Angling for Access, Bartering for Change: How Second-Stage Teachers Experience Differentiated Roles in Schools," Teachers College Record 110, no. 5: 1088–1114.

14. Johnson, S. M. and The Project on the Next Generation of Teachers. (2004). *Finders and Keepers: Helping New Teachers Survive and Thrive in Our Schools.* San Francisco: Jossey-Bass.

15. Mangin, M. M. and Stoelinga, S. R. (Eds.). (2008). *Effective Teacher Leadership: Using Research to Inform and Reform.* New York: Teachers College Press.

ABOUT THE EDITORS

CELINE COGGINS is the founder and CEO of Teach Plus. Coggins is a former teacher with experience in research and policy making. She launched Teach Plus in 2007 to rebuild the teaching profession to value teacher leadership. Since that time, the organization has grown to have a presence in six cities, working with 12,000 teachers and over 500 teacher leaders. Coggins has been a labor-management consultant in Providence, Rhode Island, as well as in Worcester and Springfield, Massachusetts, and was formerly special assistant to the Massachusetts commissioner of education on teacher quality. She has been a Mind Trust Education Entrepreneur and Aspen Institute Fellow. She is the author of several dozen reports and journal articles and the editor of two other books. She earned her PhD in education policy analysis from Stanford University.

HEATHER G. PESKE is the associate commissioner for educator quality at the Massachusetts Department of Elementary and Secondary Education, where she manages a portfolio that includes educator evaluation, preparation, and licensure. Previously she worked as the vice president of programs at Teach Plus. Peske has spent her career committed to transforming education in the United States, especially for low-income and minority students. She began as an elementary school teacher and Teach for America corps member in Baton Rouge, Louisiana. Peske earned her master's degree and doctorate in administration, planning and social policy from the Harvard Graduate School of Education. There, she was a founding member of the Project on the Next Generation of Teachers with Susan Moore Johnson. Peske has served as the director of teacher quality at The Education Trust, a national nonprofit organization dedicated to raising standards and closing achievement gaps in education. Peske is a coauthor of the award-winning book *Finders and Keepers: Helping New Teachers Survive and Thrive in Our Schools*, and has written reports and articles on teacher policy, alternative certification programs, new teachers' experiences, and conceptions of career. She graduated from Kenyon College with magna cum laude honors.

KATE MCGOVERN leads the communications strategy for Teach Plus, with a focus on ensuring that the voices of solutions-oriented urban teachers are present in the mainstream media's education dialogue. She has supported teachers to place more than 200 op-eds in major print and online publications and teaches writing and storytelling workshops to teachers nationwide. McGovern has worked in urban classrooms at home and abroad, most recently in London, and before that as a reading specialist and theater educator at the Harlem Children's Zone, where she cofounded a popular Shakespeare performance program for middle school students. Also a writer, McGovern's work has appeared in the *New York Times*, *Slate*, *Narrative Magazine*, and onstage Off-Broadway, and in 2006 she was named one of Random House's Best New Voices. McGovern earned her BA from Yale and her master's degree as a Weidenfeld Scholar at the University of Oxford.

ABOUT THE CONTRIBUTORS

TINA C. AHLGREN is a secondary school mathematics teacher at Shortridge Magnet High School for Law and Public Policy in Indianapolis, Indiana. She graduated with a bachelor's degree in mathematics and education from DePauw University. She is active at both the school and district levels, leading student groups and teacher development workshops. Ahlgren began her transformation into education activist when she was chosen as a member of the initial Indianapolis cohort of Teach Plus Teaching Policy Fellows. She has also served on the Indiana Department of Education's Reform Cabinet.

SARAH ALMY is director of teacher quality at The Education Trust. She comes to The Education Trust from TNTP, where she helped recruit, select, train, and support teachers to fill positions in high-need subjects within hard-to-staff schools. She directly oversaw TNTP's partnerships with the District of Columbia, Baltimore, Philadelphia, and Denver schools. Prior to TNTP, Almy served as executive director of Yes Reading, a nonprofit organization that partners with schools to provide structured reading interventions for students. Almy began her career as an elementary school teacher in Houston as a member of Teach for America. She holds a master's degree in policy analysis and evaluation from Stanford University and a bachelor's degree in political science from Boston College.

SUJATA BHATT is a National Board certified teacher with twelve years' experience teaching in Los Angeles Unified School District. She is the founder of The Incubator School, an innovative 6–12 pilot school focused on entrepreneurship and real-world learning. Her expertise is combining technology, arts, and creative instruction to produce a strong record of learning for high-poverty students, including gifted and special needs learners. She works closely with teachers, students, and parents to increase technological literacy and bring technological creativity into districts, classrooms, and homes through workshops, presentations, and mentoring. In addition to teaching, Bhatt is part of the founding team at Outthink Inc., a Brooklyn-based start-up that combines generative instruction, game mechanics, and mobile technology to develop apps that fuel accelerated STEM learning for 7- to 14-year-olds. She serves on the Joan Ganz Cooney Center's Games and Learning Publishing Council. She has also developed "big picture" educational policy as a Teaching Policy Fellow with Teach Plus and with Our Schools, Our Voice and Future Is Now Schools. She has written on education reform in the *Los Angeles Times*, the *Huffington Post*, and the *Washington Post*.

GINA CANEVA is in her ninth year teaching high school English in Chicago Public Schools. She began her teaching career in the Chicago Public Schools at Corliss High School in the Roseland neighborhood, where she started a school literary magazine, newspaper, and poetry slam with the help of two Oppenheimer Family Foundation grants. She also began the school's first-ever boys' volleyball team and led them to a conference championship. Caneva left Corliss after three years to become a founding teacher of TEAM Englewood Community Academy, a small high school in Englewood focused on partnering with parents and the community. There she served as English department chair and twelfth-grade lead teacher, and often led schoolwide professional development. She is now a National Board certified teacher at Lindblom Math and Science Academy and a Teach Plus Teaching Policy Fellow. She has an MEd in literacy, language, and culture from the University of Illinois at Chicago, and lives in Chicago with her husband and daughter.

DWIGHT DAVIS is an eight-year veteran teacher and a proud product of the District of Columbia Public Schools (DCPS). Currently, he serves as a fifth-grade teacher and teacher leader in DCPS, and is an alumnus of the Teach Plus Teaching Policy Fellowship. In 2011, he completed a certificate program in reading and literacy at George Washington University, and he had the distinct honor of attending the 2013 Aspen Ideas Festival as an Aspen Ideas Festival Scholar. His passion for textual relevance in literacy, teaching, and learning enables him to provide his students with the highest quality of instruction possible. In 2011 and 2012, he was a presenter at the International Reading Association Bibliotherapy Special Interest Group session. Prior to his teaching career, Davis played both professional and semiprofessional basketball in the United States and abroad (Colombia and the United Kingdom). He earned a master of divinity and a master of arts in education from Princeton Theological Seminary, as well as a BS/BA in psychology, history, and education from Albright College. Davis is a licensed Baptist minister and has served in a myriad of leadership capacities, including as president of the Association of Black Seminarians at Princeton Seminary and as student chaplain at Princeton University. He was called to serve the First Baptist Church of Hightstown in Hightstown, New Jersey, where he was the first African American to serve as pastor.

ERIN DUKESHIRE is a middle school science teacher at Orchard Gardens K–8 Pilot School in Boston. Dukeshire is also a Turnaround Teacher Team (T3) teacher leader who leads the K–8 science team, and she has taught and led her school's Summer Learning Program on Thompson Island in Boston Harbor. As a Teach Plus Teaching Policy Fellow and an America Achieves Fellow, Dukeshire collaborates with teachers from her district and across the country to advise policy makers about issues in education. She is a 2012 Massachusetts finalist for the Presidential Awards for Excellence in Mathematics and Science Teaching. Previously, Dukeshire taught science at the Academy of the Pacific Rim Public Charter School in Hyde Park, Massachusetts, and at Homestead Senior High School in Homestead, Florida, where she served with Teach for America. She is a graduate of Bowdoin College and holds a master's degree in teaching from Simmons College.

BENJAMIN FENTON is chief strategy officer and a cofounder of New Leaders. In 2000, together with several other social entrepreneurs, Fenton cofounded New Leaders, an organization dedicated to ensuring high academic achievement for all children, especially students in poverty and students of color, by developing transformational school leaders and advancing the policies and practices that allow great leaders to succeed. In his current role as chief strategy officer, Fenton leads the organization's Policy and Practice Services, helping states and districts develop new policies, strategies, and tools for principal evaluation and for improving principal effectiveness. He is also responsible for the ongoing implementation of the New Leaders' organizational learning plan and programmatic evaluation.

In previous roles at New Leaders, Fenton has served as: chief operating officer, growing the organization from a staff of 5 to more than 150 employees; chief cities officer, managing and supporting all local program sites; and chief school support officer, developing national and local strategies to support the performance of schools led by New Leaders principals. A recognized expert on principal quality, he is the lead author of the New Leaders' white papers "Principal Effectiveness" and "Evaluating Principals," and he coled the development of the Urban Excellence Framework, a detailed field guide of the school practices and principal actions found in high-gaining urban public schools.

Fenton is also a founding board member of Teach Plus. Formerly, he worked as a consultant at McKinsey and Company, focusing on marketing and operational efficiency. Fenton is a graduate of Harvard College and the Harvard Business School, where he received the Fiske award for excellence in teaching in the Economics Department.

ALLISON FRIEZE is the fourth- and fifth-grade math inclusion teacher at E. L. Haynes Public Charter School in Washington, DC. Previously, she taught third- to fifth-grade special education students in the District of Columbia Public Schools. Frieze was a 2009 DC Teaching Fellow and received awards, including Finalist, Fellow of the Year and Highly Effective Educator, under DC's IMPACT system. Frieze was a Teach Plus Teaching Policy Fellow in the 2012–2013 DC cohort. She holds a BA in Russian from Georgetown University and is pursuing an MA in early childhood special education from the George Washington University.

KATI HAYCOCK is one of the nation's leading advocates in the field of education. She currently serves as president of The Education Trust. Established in 1996, The Education Trust works for the high academic achievement of all students at all levels, prekindergarten through college. The organization's goal is to close the gaps in opportunity and achievement that consign too many low-income students and students of color to lives on the margins of the American mainstream.

Before coming to The Education Trust, Haycock served as executive vice president of the Children's Defense Fund, the nation's largest child advocacy organization.

A native Californian, Haycock founded and served as president of The Achievement Council, a statewide organization that provided assistance in improving student achievement to teachers and principals in predominantly minority schools. She also served as director of the Outreach and Student Affirmative Action programs for the nine-campus University of California system.

Kati Haycock speaks about educational improvement before thousands of educators, community and business leaders, and policy makers each year. She has received numerous awards for her service on behalf of our nation's youth, and serves as a director on several education-related boards, including the Carnegie Foundation for the Advancement of Teaching, TNTP, the Hunt Institute, and Teach Plus.

JAIME SIEBRASE HUDGINS, a Teach Plus Teaching Policy Fellowship alum, currently teaches high school history in the Memphis City Schools district. A graduate of the George Washington University, Catholic University, and Western Governors University, she has served on the iCivics Teacher's Council and currently coaches her school's policy debate team. She has been selected as a Goethe-Institut Transatlantic Outreach Program participant and traveled to Germany in June 2013 to experience, alongside other adventures, the German education system.

KYLE HUNSBERGER is a secondary school mathematics teacher at Johnnie L. Cochran Jr. Middle School, in Los Angeles, California. Hunsberger received a BS in mathematics from Wheaton College (Illinois) in 2004 and an MA in secondary education from Loyola Marymount University in 2006. In addition to serving in various leadership capacities at Cochran Middle School, Hunsberger also participated in the drafting of the Los

Angeles Unified School District (LAUSD) Teaching & Learning Framework and served as a 2011 Teach for America / LAUSD Summer Fellow and a 2012–2013 Teach Plus Teaching Policy Fellow. In 2013 Hunsberger completed an MA in educational leadership from Teachers College, Columbia University.

AUDREY HERZIG JACKSON is currently working toward a master's degree in human development and psychology at the Harvard Graduate School of Education on a Conant Fellowship, after which she will return to the classroom. Jackson taught fifth grade in Boston Public Schools for six years, specializing in teaching in a full-inclusion setting to meet the needs of all students, particularly those who have experienced trauma or who have emotional disabilities. She believes public education is one of the most powerful forms of social justice, and that all students should be part of a school community that believes in their potential and supports their growth, no matter how many challenges they face. Prior to teaching, Jackson worked on a three-year federal grant for the Isabella Stewart Gardner Museum. She researched how elementary school students develop critical thinking skills through discussions about art. Jackson incorporates her love of creativity and self-empowerment into her work and culminates each year with a week-long trip to a farm in Vermont. She earned her BA from Williams College and her MEd in elementary and special education through Boston Teacher Residency. Jackson hopes to further develop her expertise in working with children who have experienced trauma within an inclusion setting and to create resources for other educators and schools.

JASON KAMRAS currently serves as the chief of human capital for the District of Columbia Public Schools (DCPS). In this role, he leads the district's efforts to ensure that its teachers, school leaders, and central office staff members are the most effective in the nation.

Prior to this appointment, Kamras served as the director of teacher human capital for DCPS. In this position, he led the development of the IMPACT performance management system as well as the IMPACTplus performance-based compensation system. He also helped negotiate the district's groundbreaking contract with the Washington Teachers' Union.

Before joining the central office, Kamras taught mathematics for eight years at John Philip Sousa Middle School in the DCPS. Kamras began teaching in 1996 as a member of Teach for America and was named National Teacher of the Year by President Bush in 2005. Kamras holds a bachelor's degree in public policy from Princeton University and a master's degree in education from the Harvard Graduate School of Education.

TERRENCE KNEISEL is a director of city external relations support at New Leaders. In this role, he has supported development teams on fund-raising efforts in all eight city sites where New Leaders operates their program; has project-managed a successful Investing in Innovation (i3) grant application; and has overseen the organization's marketing and communications work. Prior to joining New Leaders, Kneisel spent five years on staff at Teach for America, serving first as a director of development in their Baltimore region and then as a director of talent recruitment, working to recruit potential staff members from over a dozen regions over his time in that role. Kneisel started in education as a Teach for America corps member, having taught sixth-grade reading and writing at a middle school on the Navajo reservation in New Mexico. He studied English and political science at Loyola University in Maryland and was a finalist in the New York Times 2007 Nicholas Kristof Win-a-Trip contest for educators.

LISA GONCALVES LAVIN works at Orchard Gardens K–8 Pilot School in the Boston Public Schools as a literacy interventionist and was trained as a Reading Recovery teacher. Previously she taught first-grade Sheltered English Immersion at the Blackstone Elementary School in Boston and was a member of the Turnaround Teacher Team (T3) cohort. Her other experience includes teaching in Natick, Framingham, and Cambridge, Massachusetts, in diverse classroom settings. These varied experiences inspired Goncalves to become a Teach Plus Teaching Policy Fellow in the 2011–2012 cohort. She is proficient in Portuguese and Spanish, and holds a master's degree in education and child development from Tufts University and a bachelor's degree in psychology and Spanish from the College of the Holy Cross.

EDWARD LIU, director of organizational learning for Boston Teacher Residency and Boston Plan for Excellence, is a native of Seattle, Washington. He has been a high school history teacher in Oregon, a founder and codirector of a Summerbridge (Breakthrough Collaborative) program, and an assistant professor of educational administration (at Rutgers, The State University of New Jersey). Liu holds a BA in history from Yale University, an MBA and AM in education from Stanford University, and a doctorate in education from the Harvard Graduate School of Education. At Harvard he was an original member of the Project on the Next Generation of Teachers, which conducts research addressing critical questions about the future of the nation's teaching force. He is coauthor of *Finders and Keepers: Helping New Teachers Survive and Thrive in Our Schools* (Jossey-Bass, 2004) and has been published in numerous scholarly journals.

JEANETTE MARRONE is in her seventh year of teaching and is chair of the French department at Environmental Science and Technology High School in Los Angeles. She is a faculty adviser for a federal i3 technology grant, which seeks to integrate technology skills in the classroom. She also serves on the teacher advisory panel for a grant from the Bill and Melinda Gates Foundation called The College-Ready Promise. She has a multiple-subject California Clear Credential and a Clear Credential in French. Marrone is a 2007 alumna of Teach for America—Los Angeles and has held a school board fellowship with the Los Angeles Unified School District (LAUSD) and the Teach Plus Teaching Policy Fellowship. She graduated magna cum laude from Boston College in 2007 with degrees in political science and French.

KAREN L. MCCARTHY is a National Board certified high school English teacher and special educator in the Boston Public Schools. She has worked with middle school children on Martha's Vineyard, taught math and reading to children in Guatemala, written for Let's Go Travel Guide in Spain and Portugal, and written book reviews for Teacher's College Press. McCarthy is currently in her eleventh year of teaching at Brighton High School, where she has served as a teacher leader, a Boston Teachers Union building representative, and on her school's Instructional Leadership Team and

School Site Council. In her work as a teacher leader, she mentored new and beginning teachers and worked with a team to design and facilitate professional development for her school. McCarthy has also worked with Boston Teacher Residency as a mentor, site director, and teacher of graduate courses. She has been a recipient of the Sontag Prize in Urban Education and the United Way's 2010 Teachers Rock award and is a former Teach Plus Teaching Policy Fellow. McCarthy earned a BA in English from the University of Massachusetts at Amherst and a master's degree in education from Harvard University. She is currently pursuing an MEd in educational leadership from Teachers College, Columbia University.

MICHELLE MORRISSEY teaches history at the Academy of the Pacific Rim High School (APR) in Hyde Park, Massachusetts, where she chairs the history department and serves as a member of the school's Academic Council. Morrissey also currently sits on the Boston Foundation's Teacher Advisory Board and is an alumna of the Teach Plus Teaching Policy Fellowship. Prior to coming to APR, Morrissey was a founding teacher at Teachers Preparatory High School in New York City, where she also served as the school's United Federation of Teachers chapter leader. She has also worked as a union organizer with a progressive health care union in Connecticut. Morrissey earned her BA with honors in history from Columbia University and her MA in education from Brooklyn College (CUNY) through the New York City Teaching Fellows program.

MEAGHAN PETERSACK is a second-grade teacher at Two Rivers Public Charter School in Washington, DC, and a Teach Plus Teaching Policy Fellow. She began her teaching career as a Teach for America corps member in Washington, DC. Petersack has taught kindergarten through fourth grade over the past five years in DC charter schools. Outside of the classroom, Petersack has worked with Teach for America's Social Entrepreneurship Initiative to develop teachers' ideas to close the achievement gap. In June of 2012, she completed a four-year term as a trustee of Princeton University. Petersack received her master's degree in early childhood education from George Mason University in 2010, and she holds a BA in public policy from the Woodrow Wilson School at Princeton University.

JEREMY ROBINSON teaches eleventh-grade American literature and composition at Rauner College Prep, a campus of the Chicago-based Noble Network of Charter Schools. In addition to helping his students develop a love of literature and language, Robinson leads the Junior Grade Level Team, coaches the girls' and boys' cross-country team, and serves as the adviser for a group of tenth-grade boys. Robinson's career as an educator started in 2004 at Harper High School on Chicago's South Side, where he taught ninth-grade English as a member of Teach for America. At Harper, Robinson developed a passion for promoting educational equity and improving access to college for all children—issues that continue to be at the heart of his work as a teacher. During the summer of 2011, he served as an Urban Leaders Fellow in the office of Colorado State Senator Mike Johnston while also interning at DSST (Denver School of Science and Technology) Public Schools. A current Teach Plus Chicago Teaching Policy Fellow, Robinson has a bachelor's degree from Wabash College and master's degrees from Dominican University and the University of Oxford.

LINDSAY SOBEL is the executive director of Teach Plus Greater Boston. Before becoming executive director, Sobel served as the first director of the Teach Plus Network, providing thousands of teachers around the country with opportunities to learn, connect, and make an impact for their students. Prior to Teach Plus, Sobel launched the 8th Grade Academy writing program and the Science and Technology Initiative at Citizen Schools, an organization focused on expanding the learning day for low-income middle school students.

Sobel started her career as a political journalist, helping to launch *Slate* magazine, covering Congress for *The Hill*, and founding the *American Prospect*'s online political magazine. She has also served as an adjunct journalism professor at Emerson College. Sobel holds a BA from the University of Michigan and an MPP from the Harvard Kennedy School.

PETER TANG currently teaches at Westside Middle School in Tennessee's Achievement School District, where he transitioned in the 2013–2014 school year to help it achieve the goal of moving the bottom 5 percent of Tennessee's students to the top 25 percent in five years. Prior to joining Westside Middle School, Tang taught seventh-grade math at Kate

Bond Middle School in Memphis City Schools, where he served as the math department chairperson, on the Site-Based Decision Making Council, and as an assistant coach for the girls' soccer team. During his first year as a 2010 Teach for America corps member, he taught eleventh-grade English at East High School in Memphis City Schools, and previously he also taught in an English-immersion program in Hong Kong. Tang currently serves as a Common Core coach for math to support Tennessee teachers transitioning to the Common Core. Outside of the classroom, he is a Teaching Policy Fellow with Teach Plus and a fellow with Humanity in Action, an international educational organization. A native of Brooklyn, New York, Tang received his bachelor of arts in history from Amherst College.

MONIQUE BURNS THOMPSON has been president of Teach Plus since its incorporation in 2009. She brings experience as a social entrepreneur, management and human capital consultant, and reform-oriented district administrator to the Teach Plus team. She started her career in the business sector (Quaker Oats Company) in marketing and brand management before moving to the education sector as a consultant for The McKenzie Group, Incorporated, opening model middle schools in Washington, DC. After spending a year as the assistant principal of one of those schools, Burns Thompson worked as special assistant to the superintendent of the Philadelphia Public School District, which informed her understanding of the need for quality training of urban school teachers and leaders. This focus on human capital development led her to cofound and colead New Leaders for New Schools (now New Leaders) as president and chief curriculum officer. She later worked as a consultant for districts and charter organizations striving to develop school-based leadership capacities. Burns Thompson earned her bachelor's degree from Dartmouth College, her MBA from Harvard Business School, and her master's in education from Harvard Graduate School of Education. She is ABD for her doctorate in education administration and social policy.

PAUL TONER, president of the 110,000-member Massachusetts Teachers Association (MTA), is a strong voice for educators and a proud public school parent. Toner is dedicated to working on behalf of students at all levels and to representing the interests of teachers, education support professionals, and higher education faculty and staff.

A middle school social studies teacher, lawyer, and former president of the Cambridge Teachers Association, Toner was elected MTA president after serving for four years as the association's vice president. From 1993 to 2001, Toner taught social studies and reading to seventh- and eighth-grade students at the Harrington Elementary School in Cambridge.

Toner was named a Teacher Leader Fellow by the Aspen Institute, and he has been appointed by NEA President Dennis Van Roekel to several National Education Association committees focused on leading the profession and digital learning. Toner was recently elected president of the National Council of State Education Association and served as chair of Mass Partners for Public Schools, a coalition of organizations representing superintendents, principals, teacher unions, and parents, and is active in the Teacher Union Reform Network, a national group that has sought to develop and share teacher-led school improvement practices at the local level. He is a member of the Massachusetts 2020 Expanded Learning Time Advisory Board. He served on the Massachusetts Board of Elementary and Secondary Education's Educator Evaluation Task Force, Task Force on 21st Century Skills, and Task Force on Closing the Proficiency Gap. He also was a participant in Governor Deval Patrick's Readiness Project. He is an appointed member of the Massachusetts Board of Higher Education. He is a labor delegate to the Democratic State Committee (DSC) and a member of the DSC Executive Committee.

Toner graduated from Boston University's College of Liberal Arts with a bachelor's degree in political science and international relations. He also holds a master's degree in secondary education from the University of Massachusetts Boston. While teaching full-time, Toner earned his juris doctorate from Suffolk University Law School at night.

STEPHANIE WIDMER joined the teaching profession through Teach for America in 2007. She taught sixth-grade English, ESL, and history at Nightingale Middle School, Los Angeles, where she also cocoached the school's Students Run LA team. She then taught at New Los Angeles Charter School, teaching sixth- and seventh-grade humanities. From there, she spent two years coaching and developing teachers as a manager of Teacher Leadership Development for Teach for America. She continues to work with Teach for America as a Professional Learning Community facilitator and has spent several summers leading teams at the Teach for America Summer Institute as both a corps member adviser and school director. Widmer currently teaches eighth-grade humanities at Camino Nuevo Charter Academy—Harvard, Los Angeles, where she is focusing on high school readiness, rigor, and reader's and writer's workshop with her students. She received her BA in philosophy from Scripps College and her MA from Loyola Marymount University. She is a Teach Plus Los Angeles Teaching Policy Fellow.

ROSS WIENER is a vice president at the Aspen Institute and executive director of the Education and Society Program. In this role, Wiener leads professional learning networks for urban school district leaders and senior congressional education staffers. The program assists policy makers and education leaders in strengthening human capital systems, supporting implementation of Common Core State Standards, and strategically reallocating financial resources.

In addition to facilitating networks, the Education and Society Program hosts public conversations as well as off-the-record workshops, and publishes original research and commentary. From 2002 to 2009, Wiener worked at The Education Trust, a national nonprofit organization dedicated to raising standards and closing achievement gaps in public education. As policy director and then as vice president for program and policy, Wiener managed The Education Trust's research/data analysis, policy development, conference programming, and technical assistance to educators and policy makers in both K–12 and higher education.

Prior to The Education Trust, Wiener served for five years as a trial attorney in the U.S. Department of Justice, Civil Rights Division, Educational Opportunities Section, where he represented the United States in cases dealing with desegregation, harassment, and the adequacy of services to limited-English-proficient and disabled students.

INDEX

accountability, 2, 5, 37, 52, 69, 117
achievement gaps, 2, 8, 37, 40, 51
adequate yearly progress, 69
African American students, 2, 80
American Federation of Teachers (AFT), 85, 109, 110
arts, 51
Aspire Public Schools, 19
assessment data, 16–17, 50–51, 53, 66
attrition rates, 2, 57, 89–90, 113

baby boomer retirements, 56, 67, 70
bar exams, 109–110
behavior management, 43
benchmark assessments, 16

career ladders, 82, 102, 111–114, 121–122
charter schools, 64, 96–98, 101
class sizes, 83
coaching support, 89
collaboration, 25, 37, 45, 48–49, 54, 83, 93, 99
Common Core State Standards, 2–3, 12, 16, 50
compensation, 39, 53, 67, 81–83, 118–119, 122–123

data
  access to, 6
  analysis, 9
  assessment, 16–17, 50–51, 53, 66
  observation, 17
  standardized tests, 10–13
  student achievement, 6
  student progress, 6, 13–15
  on teacher effectiveness, 21–22
  use of, 5–19, 31
  value-added, 6, 13–14, 44–46, 53
data-driven decision making, 18, 31
decision making
  data-driven, 18, 31
  parent, 12
  performance-based, 40
  seniority-driven, 55–68
  teacher-driven, 31
demographic shifts, 1–2, 56–57, 67, 70
disadvantaged students, access to quality teachers by, 21–38

early career teachers. *See* novice teachers
education governance, 2
education policies, 69–70, 72–73, 105–106, 127
education reform, 78–80, 105–106
effectiveness estimates, 6
Elementary and Secondary Education Act, 22, 69
emotionally impaired (EI) students, 92–94
entry standards, 3, 108–111, 115–119
evaluation systems
  anxiety over, 47
  comprehensive, 50–51, 66
  IMPACT, 39, 44–46, 49, 53, 54, 89
  implementation of, 50–52

evaluation systems, *continued*
inadequacies of, 63–64
need for effective, 37–38, 39, 41–43
new, 2–3
for principals, 103
role of teacher voice in, 48–49, 54
student assessment and, 6, 21, 44–46, 50–51, 66
trust in, 50–51, 54
value-added model, 6, 13–17, 44–46, 53
expectations, 31–32, 37, 51, 101

feedback, to teachers, 17, 31–32, 37, 41–46, 100–101
female-dominated professions, 106–107

generational change, 1–2, 56–57, 70, 83–84
Generation Y teachers, 57

high-poverty schools
accountability in, 69
layoffs in, 67–68
seniority system and, 63–65
teacher quality and, 21–23
human capital, 54, 99

IMPACT, 39, 44–46, 49, 53, 54, 89
incentives, 5
inclusive teaching, 92–94
Individual Value Added (IVA), 44–46
See also value-added model
ineffective teaching, 21, 81
See also teacher effectiveness
Instructional Leadership Team (ILT), 29
interim assessment, 16, 18

last in, first out (LIFO) policies, 55–68
Latino students, 2
layoffs, 39, 56, 58–68
leadership
cultivating, 102
opportunities, 3, 56–57, 102, 113–114, 121–122
pathways to, 82
principal, 92–94, 99–104
roles, 34
school, 37, 87–104
shared, 30–31, 35, 37
teacher, 25–35, 102, 113–114, 121–122, 127
union, 73–76, 84–86
licensing requirements, 108–111, 116, 120
low-income students, teacher quality and, 21–23, 36–38, 67–68
low-poverty schools, 21

Massachusetts Comprehensive Assessment System (MCAS), 12
Measures of Effective Teaching project, 50
minority students, teacher quality and, 21–23
motivation, 9

National Assessment of Educational Progress (NAEP), 73
National Education Association, 85
Noble Network, 96–98, 101
No Child Left Behind, 1, 10
nontraditional teaching candidates, 116
novice teachers
assigment to high-poverty schools, 21
attitudes of, 1–2
entry and training standards for, 3, 108–111, 115–124
layoffs of, 58–59, 62–65
residency programs for, 117, 120–121

support for, 41–43, 90–91
teacher unions and, 69–86

observation data, 17

parent decision making, 12
parents, 93
pay scales, 81–82, 118–119, 122–123
peer observers, 3, 17
pensions, 67
performance-based compensation, 39, 53, 81–82, 83, 118–119
performance-driven profession, 55–68
physical education, 51
politics, 125
Praxis teaching exams, 109
principal-as-coach model, 42
principals, 87–104
professional development, 18, 25, 45, 47, 50, 118
professional growth, 37
professionalism, 3
professional learning communities, 18
professional support systems, 50
See also teacher support
public sector jobs, 80

quality-blind staffing policies, 55–68
quality teachers
See also teacher effectiveness; teacher quality
effect of, 21, 40, 53, 55
equitable access to, 21–38
turnaround schools and, 24–35
quantified self, 9–10

Race to the Top, 54, 72–73, 84

Reality PD, 45
recruitment practices, 101–102, 115–117, 123
research-based structures, 31
residency programs, 117, 120–121
retention, teacher, 88–91, 103–104

school administration, 42, 50, 54, 87–104
school-based teacher leader teams, 29–30
school culture, 34, 91, 99–101, 126
school leadership, 37, 87–104
schools of education, 117–118
seniority-driven orientation, 55–68
shared leadership, 30–31, 35, 37
socioeconomic status, 8, 51
staff cohesion, 37
staffing decisions, 58–68
stakeholders, 69–71
standardized tests, 7–8, 10–13, 16–17, 31–32
standards movement, 2
state tests. *See* standardized tests
step-and-lane systems, 67, 81–82
student achievement
data, 6
evaluation systems and, 6, 21, 44–46, 50–51, 66
impact of teacher effectiveness on, 21, 40, 53
measurement of, 8, 10–13, 16–17, 50–51, 53
principal's role in, 87, 103
student assessment, 16–17, 50–51, 53, 66
student progress data, 6, 13–15
student teachers, 117

T3 Initiative. *See* Turnaround Teacher Teams (T3) Initiative
teacher advocacy, 60–62

teacher collaboration, 45, 48–49, 54, 83, 93, 99
teacher-driven decision making, 31
teacher education, 108–111, 115–118
teacher effectiveness
data on, 5–6, 21–22
impact of, on student achievement, 21, 40, 53, 55
measurement of, 5, 6, 14–15, 22–23, 37, 39–54, 66
principal's role in, 87–104
seniority-driven orientation and, 66–67
Teacher Effectiveness Initiative, 47–52
Teacher Effectiveness Measure (TEM), 48–52
teacher evaluation systems. *See* evaluation systems
teacher leadership, 25–35, 102, 113–114, 121–122, 127
teacher-led school change, 26–27
teacher placement, 58–68
teacher preparation, 105–124
teacher quality
See also teacher effectiveness
disparities in, 21–23, 39–40
focus on, 105–106
research on variations in, 56–57
staffing decisions and, 58–68
teachers
See also novice teachers; quality teachers; veteran teachers
access to great, 21–38
attitudes of new, 1–2
career ladders for, 82, 102, 111–114, 121–122
data use by, 5–19
entry and training standards for, 105–124
expectations for, 31–32, 37, 51, 101
recruitment of, 101–102, 115–117, 123
retention of, 88–91, 103–104
role of, 105–106
standards for, 22, 108–111
status of, 105–124
temporary, 57, 64
teacher strikes, 80
teacher support, 18–19, 37, 41–43, 50, 54, 89–91, 103
teacher unions, 69–86
teacher voice, 125–127
Teach for America, 95–96, 109, 111, 123
Teaching and Learning Framework (TLF), 44–46
teaching profession
changes in, 1–4
changing to performance-driven, 55–68
entry standards for, 115–119
status of, 105–124
Teach Plus, 2, 3, 26, 36, 41, 48–49, 125
Teach Plus Teaching Policy Fellows, 60–61
temporary teachers, 57, 64
TenMarks, 8–9
tenure systems, 55–68, 79, 81
test scores, 6, 8, 10–13, 16–17, 44–46, 66
trust, 30–31, 42, 46–47, 91, 103–104
turnaround schools, 24–35, 36
Turnaround Teacher Teams (T3) Initiative, 3, 24–35, 36, 113
turnover rates, 2, 89–90, 113

urban school systems, 2, 89–90, 113
See also high-poverty schools

value-added model, 6, 13–17, 44–46, 53
veteran teachers
retirement of, 70
seniority-based decisions and, 55–68
unions and, 70–71

work environment, 37